PLAY WORLD

PLAY WORLD

The Emergence of the New Ludenic Age

James E. Combs

Westport, Connecticut
London

Library of Congress Cataloging-in-Publication Data

Combs, James E.
    Play world : the emergence of the new ludenic age / James E. Combs.
       p. cm.
    Includes bibliographical references and index.
    ISBN 0–275–96838–3 (alk. paper)
    1. Play—History. 2. Play—Sociological aspects—History. I. Title.
GV14.45.C63 2000
306.4′81—dc21   00–022344

British Library Cataloguing in Publication Data is available.

Library of Congress Catalog Card Number: 00–022344
ISBN: 0–275–96838–3

First published in 2000

Praeger Publishers, 88 Post Road West, Westport, CT 06881
An imprint of Greenwood Publishing Group, Inc.
www.praeger.com

Printed in the United States of America

Hello, Puff

Contents

Acknowledgments

The author wishes to acknowledge with many thanks the staff of the Russell County Public Library. Director Charlotte Duty, Circulation Supervisor Jean Judkins, and the rest of the able (if badly underpaid) library staff were always helpful in this endeavor. And, as always, I also want to acknowledge the constant help and support of my roommate, helpmate, and soul mate, Sara.

Introduction: The Play of Musement, and the Musement of Play

Our subject is *play*. It is customary at the onset of an inquiry into play to say something about "taking play seriously." Our approach will be slightly different: why not discuss play playfully? Playfulness is before all an *attitude*, an orientation to the world, premised by the notion that life is too important to take seriously. Playfulness can be contrasted with its antonym, *earnestness*, the attitude that life is so important that it must be taken seriously. Earnest inquiry into play often becomes dreadfully serious, as if the inquirer fears treating play playfully, and hopes to tame the spirit of play through the poison gases of weighty seriousness and grave solemnity. The attitude of earnestness (recall the term "dead earnest") in both its Latin and Gothic origins connotes "heaviness"; play, by contrast, is associated with "lightness"—merry heart, frolic, dallying, sportive, toying, laughter and funning, fooling around, carefree. The weight of earnest care includes worry and woe and all of life's burdens; when weights are lifted, our attitude becomes carefree, free to play. Let's have some fun.

Play is not just an attitudinal propensity to act, though; playfulness is the attitude that gives impetus and credence to the act of play. Play as we experience it is an *activity*, from the private daydreams of a bored student or lonely shut-in to the flow of energetic action in a game of contesting or cooperating players. The activity of play is here contrasted with activities of (to use the archaic term) *seriosity*. Play and seriosity often get mixed up and confused, since play is accorded social meaning. Play is typically a project of *active fun*, at its purest when the players experience the flow of play life apart from the mundane cares and woes of everyday life.[1] At its most memorable, play is vivacious, even ecstatic joy, from the enjoyment of private fulfillment in daydreams to the "highs" of game play. A reverie of imaginary union with your fantasy girl or guy may be just as satisfying as a touchdown or checkmate.

But we also do not live, or play, in isolation. Play is a *social activity*, fun in the context of social life. Even the lonely daydreamer is dreaming of social play, with beautiful playmates or fellow warriors or admiring colleagues. In every society play takes on *social form*. Certain kinds of play are given social legitimacy, and others are discouraged or forbidden. Children are told not to "play with fire." Play is given a definite time and place for its conduct. Social authorities also give play rules, sometimes informal but at other times quite formal. The more a kind of play is regarded as socially important, the more circumscribed it will be as to legitimacy, time and place, and rules.

Take that widespread institution most readers are familiar with: school. In the lower grades of school, we learn the distinction between playfulness ("I want to have fun") and earnestness ("I need to do things"). When we are allowed out for that period of play called recess, we are temporarily freed from the schoolroom attitude of seriosity ("Get things done") for playtime ("Have fun"). As we grow older, school play is increasingly organized ("Have our kind of good fun") but still usually distinguishable from schoolwork ("Earnest effort in the classroom is expected"). School sports often suffer from the social circumscription of play as important, but for most students the play provided by school is still fun. Indeed, what most people likely remember about school are the fun times. This may be a commentary on the dreary rituals of schoolwork, but it also tells us much about our preference for, and sweet memories of, play.

With the above opening remarks in mind, let us ask the comic muse Thalia to guide us through the elysian fields of play, with the suggestion that learning about play is best approached with a relaxed attitude of bemused playfulness that will help us understand the appeals of play and the nature of *homo ludens*. "Humankind the player" encompasses, after all, those amongst us who are *having fun*, so it seems to follow that those who write and read about play should also have a little fun in the process. Learning about play invites a sprightly and inquisitive spirit, informed by the notion that people are at their best, and most receptive to learning, when they don't take themselves or their subject matter too seriously. This is not to say that play is not important, only that it is best understood by approaching that importance in the right way. Academic tomes can be the most serious and dismal of all forms of earnest communication. But the unique subject of play suggests that rather than get serious about play, we should get playful about seriousness, and enjoy ourselves in our collaborative musement.

At this point, the reader may be tempted to think, "The message so far is, don't take this book seriously." But no: the idea here is to look at the subject of play in the light of our own experience as players, and thus our knowledge of playing. With this personal knowledge, we ought to be able to make sense of play without relying totally on the literature of play as an academic subject. Now, anyone who thinks that a subject as compelling as play cannot be made boring underestimates the power of higher education. Academic seriosity can be countered by studying play with the lighthearted spirit of what Nietzsche called "the gay science," a Dionysian spirit of gaiety in inquiry.[2]

To be sure, the consideration of anything involves a degree of energetic concentration, such as reading this book. Inquiry into play should involve alert engagement with perhaps the most delightful form of human activity. Charles Sanders Peirce's term "the play of musement" captures the attitude we recommend. "Enter your skiff of Musement," wrote Peirce, "push off into the lake of thought, and leave the breath of heaven to swell your sail. With your eyes open, awake to what is about within you, and open conversation with yourself; for such is all meditation."[3] Our injunction, then, is not "Don't take this seriously" but rather "Let us play with the idea of play." Musing over the meaning and practice of play might even teach us something significant about ourselves and the world.

PLAY AND EXISTENCE: OR WHEN IS IT RECESS?

Let us elaborate by looking at the primary, and perhaps ultimate, players: children. Now, it is important to understand child's play, since that is the period of our lives when we *learn to play*, and more importantly, *learn from play*. We still respond with horror to Dickensian tales of childhood in which contemporary Oliver Twists are deprived of childhood play by sweatshops or war. But we also wring our hands when we discover that children are learning all kinds of things we think they shouldn't be learning. At early ages, kids figure out and are much interested in things they shouldn't know or say or

do. When a child does something shocking, it is often discovered that
he or she thought what they were doing—tormenting a playmate,
setting fire to the house, poisoning a teacher—was "just" play. The
child's fantasy life, including experience with popular culture, blurs
the distinction between an earnest act of real consequences and a
playful act of unreal fantasy and thus no consequences. A good bit of
the "No, no" and "Stop that" imperatives spoken by adults are directed toward making children aware of the real consequences of
play ("No, no, you can't hold your sister's head under water"). Children soon learn that the adult world is one of earnest imperatives
and heavy responsibilities, of all kinds of things you can't do and
shouldn't do and must do. A lot of that "socialization" involves the
regulation or suppression of playing. "You can't play now; it's time
for you to do your homework, clean up your room, practice your piano." "Come in to supper; you have to stop playing and sit at the dinner table and be miserable while the adults talk about dumb things
and correct your behavior." Perhaps a lot of our resistance to growing
up and abandoning a life of play stems from our realization as children that if they get their way, we'll wind up being like *them*,
playless and resolutely earnest adults.[4]

The purpose of socialization, then, is to make the child act like an
adult, which includes abandoning the primary joy of childhood: playing. The eternal appeal of the recognition scene at the end of the
great American film *Citizen Kane* speaks to all of us: the great man
Kane, disappointed in adult life, remembers with tearful nostalgia a
treasured object of childhood play. And indeed, it is a common human
fantasy to attribute to our remembered childhood a mythic status as
a special and happier time, in which the cares and woes of adulthood
were absent and we spent golden days devoting ourselves to playing.
For many this may be a phantasm that excludes from memory the
times of childhood pain and ennui and worry. But it is a nice and un-
derstandable fantasy, as evidenced by the bitterness of those who for
some reason had a terrible childhood and often pamper their own
children, hoping they never grow up.

But as adults, we tend to have an ambivalent attitude toward the
enjoyment of childhood play. Even though we may be nostalgic for it,
regress into childish behavior ourselves, and enjoy watching children at play, we also go to great lengths to control and even end play.
The messages "Act your age" and "Behave yourself" are recognized
by the child as an injunction to act like an adult, which for them
means not like a child at play. When an adolescent or adult does
something deemed "childish," the message of approbation often is,

"Oh, grow up." The hijinks of men—usually deemed "boys" or "buddies"—in groups (fraternities, armies, friends) that tend to the idiotic are condemned as "infantile" or "adolescent" or "sophomoric." Women in groups suffer the same charge: together, they become giggly "girls" who abandon adult restraints for the delights of "immature" gossipy girl talk and action, in other words, saying and doing things that adults shouldn't but kids do, playing around, fooling around, and having fun. On the other hand, we celebrate getting in touch with our "inner child" and engage in childish behavior—playing games, having affairs, laughing hysterically, daydreaming, and skipping work. We deem childish regressions as irresponsible, an abandonment of adulthood. But our experience with childhood reminds us that child's play was fun, and at moments of reverie or weakness or conviviality, we enjoy escaping for a time into a state of playfulness. Adult responsibility—the message from others and self to contain desire, quell spontaneity, stifle gaiety, suppress enjoyment—is sometimes too much to bear.

As social beings, we learn all too quickly that society expects us to behave. We understand what we might term the *demarcation of play*. Long ago, communications scholar Gregory Bateson watched the monkeys in the San Francisco zoo and noticed that they communicated to each other a behavioral pattern with rules or codes the simian participants understood. He called this understood pattern "metacommunication." The monkeys were engaged in a form of behavior we name "play"; in their own abbadabbadabba monkey talk, they communicated to each other the operational message "This is play." What they were going to do was not fighting, so was not "serious"; rather they were going to fool around within the rules of the monkey game. Once it was established that they were going to play, what they did afterward was demarcated as play, and thus they wrestled and fought without hurting each other.[5] From a very early age, humans understand and communicate the demarcation of play, when and where it is legitimate and permitted and encouraged (and also where it is not). As a form of behavior, we set boundaries and discrete limits on the setting and conduct of play.

To adult observers, the play of kittens or small children seems to be anarchic, random behaviors that are enthusiastic but unfocused and undirected. But in the process, the kittens and kids are *learning* how to behave in the cat and human interaction order. As cats and children age, they learn through play, and they learn *how to play*. Anarchic play becomes informally more organized, and eventually formally organized in *games*, or play with demarcations and rules:

"Play goes on here within these boundaries, and by these rules." The higher mammals and humans recognize the behavioral code that announces, "This is play." The behavioral rule to be understood is, "Now we are playing, so let us play, so here's what we're playing, and here's how to play." Major misunderstandings and conflicts occur when the message—the "metacommunication"—of play isn't understood. For example, a common form of play is conversational—joking or kidding around, playful repartee that is often derogatory or humiliating. Young males and females in locker rooms often poke fun at the physical condition of the bodies they see, but if someone is "not in on" the jokes about physiques, they may be puzzled or take offense if they are the butt (as it were) of a deprecating joke. Similarly, graduate students often play intellectual games that amount to displays of "one-upmanship," showing off and competing over their intellectual sharpness or superior knowledge. An outsider may think all this a bit silly, but for those "inside" the interaction order of the locker room or graduate dorm, such play is important. In both cases, play may well serve to establish or reinforce a hierarchy, bind relations, or degrade those who are deemed inferior. Oftentimes "harmless play" is not so harmless, but if it is not taken seriously by the parties concerned, it may simply be a relaxing interlude in the conduct of the day.

People also learn at an early age the *definition of play*. Since there is a social world of earnest seriousness, institutional duties, and social responsibilities, we learn not only how to demarcate play in time and place, but also define what it is. When we say "This is play," we need to know what we're talking about. Playing around in the wrong context—making jokes about crashing to a planeload of first-time flyers, laughing at something that everyone else is taking seriously—can be embarrassing or even threatening. Making racial or ethnic jokes within hearing of an urban street gang can be bad for your health. So it is important to understand *the definition of the play situation*. To paraphrase a famous dictum, if people define situations as play, they are playful in their consequences. When we define what we are doing as "fun," from private daydreaming to deciding with others on, say, an impromptu road trip or a plan to play rugby in a school league, we believe we are going to get something out of it. If we have defined the situation as play, we hope to enjoy ourselves, and are quite disappointed when it turns out to be "no fun."

Thus in ambiguous situations where we are not sure what is happening, we ask, "Is this play?" If, when awaiting our first lecture in a class on, say, political philosophy—a subject we might have thought forbidding—the professor turns out to be a jokester telling funny stories and making puns, we may furtively ask ourselves, "Is this allowed? Isn't school and this class supposed to be a pain?" But if this jaunty beginning settles down into the routines of lectures and exams and textbook reading, the brief hope that the class could be fun is dashed by the norms of institutional seriosity. If classes are called off for some reason, there is suddenly the opportunity for play. When that happens, people may begin to ask, in effect, "May we now play?" If an encounter with someone you are attracted to at a party turns out well, you are delighted with your playful good fortune: you and your new friend are now playing ("OK, we like each other, so let's play some more"). But if not, you are beset by that dreadful question, "Are we having fun yet?" And if an encounter turns out to be unfortunate, the defining conclusion is, "(S)he's no fun."

So what we typically want out of playful relationships is fun. One great scholar, William Stephenson, referred to this as *communication-pleasure*: "I shall consider all work to be communication-pain (work gets something done), and all play to be communication-pleasure (play is just fun). . . . I shall consider all social control to veer toward communication-pain, and all convergent selectivity to veer toward communication-pleasure."[6] Work is earnest effort toward some serious purpose deemed worthy of the pain involved, and play is nonearnest activity deemed worth doing because it gives pleasure. A private fantasy communicates to oneself some fanciful desire, evoking pleasurable images and sensations; a party or road trip may make for pleasurable communications in conversational interactions such as flirting and joke telling and gossip; even playing a structured game such as rugby, with all of its intense effort and physical pain ("Give blood. Play rugby"), brings pleasure through enjoyment of the physical clash and the thrill of the contest. We must add that not all play is pleasurable to everyone. Professional athletes may view what they do as a job and hard work rather than something that brings exultant joy, and some who watch a game such as a Super Bowl may find it a big bore. And for those who are incapable of letting loose and having fun, play is petty silliness and a waste of time.

So we learn in social experience the demarcation of play (when and where it happens, and is appropriate) and the definition of play (what it is and what we are supposed to get out of it). In the process, we also learn the *social meaning of play*—in a sense, why it happens. You might be tempted to think that play is merely fooling around, consisting of trifling diversions and meaningless episodes in the stream of life, and that what is meaningful and important is the world of earnest endeavor—school, marriage and parenthood, career, indeed the entire web of "serious" adult relationships that one forms, as Marley's ghost says to Scrooge, the chains I forged in life. But the great analysts of play think otherwise. The Dutch historian Huizinga argued that our images of humankind cannot be restricted to *homo sapiens*, humans as rational beings, or *homo faber*, people as makers and workers, but must include *homo ludens* (from the Latin *ludus*, play or sport; the Romans referred to public spectacles and exhibitions as *ludi publici* and the theater as *ludi scenici*), humans as players. We may play in the "inter-ludes" of the day or calendar, but there, Huizinga says, is where culture is learned and created and communicated and passed on. "All play means something," he says. The "fun-element" that "characterizes the essence of play" is an "absolutely primary category of life."[7] In other words, culture, the symbolic and aesthetic aspects of social life, is given meaning in play, from the simplest kind of childhood play on a playground to the "high" play of religious and patriotic ritual. The battle of Waterloo was won on the playing fields of Eton, and anyone who has ever attended a sports banquet knows that high school varsity play is also given great social meaning (e.g., "fair play," "sportsmanship," "winning the great game of life").

Social groups give an extrinsic meaning to play—sports are a metaphor for life, recreation makes people better workers and citizens, leisure is a legitimate reward for work or wise investments or marrying well, and so on. But we as individuals also give play an intrinsic meaning: What does it mean to us? Do we in fact learn the "lessons" of play that society wants us to? Do we, for instance, learn sportsmanship and fair play from sports, or do we learn from either playing or watching play to cheat and lie and break the rules and switch teams for more money or throw childish fits or do outrageous things with the expectation of getting away with it? There are clearly both social and antisocial messages from play, approved and unapproved lessons, and often individual interpretations of what play means. It does seem certain that play has individual and social consequences, as a form of behavior that appears especially conducive to learning. It may even be the case that pleasurable play learning is more lasting than the "work learning" of family socialization and school indoctrination.

Why would this be so? Because, we think, play is more fun, and thus makes us more receptive to playful meanings and interpretations learned in fun. We may soon forget "official" facts and pay lip service to authoritative messages of what we should do and be, but we may never forget being blamed for the team loss during recess or the embarrassment of saying the wrong thing on a first date. The fun time of play can go right or wrong, but we recognize it as a special time—an interlude—of pretense and even drama. Play, said Huizinga, is "not 'ordinary' or 'real' life. It is rather a stepping out of 'real' life into a temporary sphere of activity with a disposition all its own."[8] "Play is going," note two other scholars. "It is what happens after all the decisions are made—when 'let's go' is the last thing one remembers."[9] At that point, you are approaching what has been called "deep play"[10], when you are really "into" or absorbed with play—at the point of checkmate in a chess game, with a group of partisans watching a contest at the moment the outcome hangs in the balance, furiously writing a poem, achieving "runner's high," or at the height of sexual ecstasy. Casual or "shallow" play is less intense and committed—loafing, reading the newspaper, half watching a soap opera while eating lunch, casual conversation. Yet in all cases, from daydreaming to participation in highly structured play such as a basketball team or choral group, you feel yourself in an "as if" time and place that differs from work, worry, anxiety, boredom, fear, ennui, or other states of existence. You have indeed let go. This often makes play memorable, and becomes incorporated into the meanings that we attribute to experience and remember well.

THE PLAY's THE THING

So we think play to be a transaction with our social environment in which the participants have defined the situation as play. Further, those participating in play figure out its rules and conventions, and communicate to one another that they are using the available *forms of mediation* to play. The agencies of play can range from simple daydreams of imagined fun to elaborate ritual play, but it has to be communicated ("We are now communicating play by speaking, acting, contesting, loving, marching, praying, or whatever"). And as the forms of mediation expand, we find new means and agencies of play—the Internet, the home movie camera, the mobile telephone, the fax machine, and so on. Finally, engagement in play invites performance. There is a principle of *drama* inherent in play. What is dramatized is virtually limitless—status anxieties, sexual longings, social characterizations, accounts of events, cultural solidarity, you name it. Once we have decided to "go," we seek the means of commu-

nicating with fellow players and use the resources of drama to structure our play.

A few examples will illustrate. When we daydream about someone
we desire, we structure the fantasy into a play with all of the characteristics of a drama: perhaps we portray ourselves as sexually irresistible, and imagine ourselves playing out a scene uniting us with a
fantasy mate in an intimate consummation that dramatizes our private wishes. Or take another example: telling a joke. "Have you
heard the one about . . ." signals that this is play. The joke teller uses
language and gesture to build the joking story toward the punch line,
which if told properly for the right audience produces laughter. Indeed, the dramatic principle seems to hold in all kinds of storytelling.
When we tell a story—ranging from gossip to jokes to elaborate accounts to Homeric epic poems—we become the performer who mim-
ics the real activity in a play context. The context of pretense invites
dramatic performance of the story. Although cultures may vary in
the conduct of such storytelling, most all have speech and gestural
patterns that let us "dress up" the play being reconstructed.[11]

Americans are noted for certain forms of dramatic animation in
their speech performances. As children, we would play fantasy
games after someone said, "Let's pretend or " 'tend like"—"we're soldiers or cowboys or parents," acting out the play. As young adults,
" 'tend like" comes out as "like" stories, as in an account such as, "He
goes, 'Why didn't you call me?' and I'm like, 'I can't believe this is happening,' " accompanied by gestures that act out the miniplay—mock
astonishment, rolling eyes, changing voice inflections to mimic the
auditors, gestures of amazement and other emotions, and so on. This
speech performance is the "kind of talk (that) attempts to show
rather than tell" wherein the "story is not reported so much as it is
rendered." Such showy rendering enhances the histrionic quality of
the "play-like" being performed. So when people perform "like" stories, they are, like, acting *too* showy and maybe *overdoing it* in their
performance, you *know* what I'm saying? As both children and
adults, we tend to translate experience into dramaturgy, in this case
a form of "oral poetry," making sense of the world by rendering it in
the context of the "as if" or "like" world of imaginative reconstruction. But then, theater at any level of performance appeals to illusion
(from *illudere*), meaning "in-play."[12]

Too, theater at any level—from informal talk to formal theatrical
productions—is a social event involving performance before or with
an audience, a relationship wherein everyone is aware of the norms
of cultural performing and is capable of evaluating the role perform-

ance of everyone acting in the play-drama. This can range from a pickup basketball game in a city park to a blind date to a moot court debate. One observer of play has noted that play behavior is "affective," activity in the "simulative mode" involving symbolic acts that assume a "nonliteral attitude."[13] Play-dramas can proceed when the parties to the transaction tacitly agree that what is being said or done is not what it appears to be, not "the real thing," the literal truth, or anything more than "pretend like." The person performing the "like" minidrama is conjuring up the in-play illusion that their simulation of what was said is "like" what happened only through their dramatic interpretation. In that sense, play is not "true" or not "meant." (If someone takes offense at a playful remark, the apology usually is a disclaimer: "I was just funning" or "I didn't mean it," although sometimes the response is an accusation: "You're no fun" or "You can't take a joke" or "Don't you have a sense of humor?") Play occurs in what Erving Goffman calls a "frame," wherein playing involves the intrusion of unserious mimicry during interaction.[14] If actors and audience agree upon the nonliteral orientation, the context of pretense, and the conduct of simulated action, then play can proceed. The players and spectators understand that what is being said and done is not what it might appear to be to an uninformed outsider. In-play, the actors and auditors occupy a "like" world of enchanted communication, unlike the earnest world of reality. When you say, "let's play," you can tell a story by mimicking the actors, but it's not a put-down, just a put-on.

We should note that play is further complicated when at least one party to the relationship is acting in bad faith, most infamously when one actor defines it as a con. The confidence man or woman, or con artist, is playing a different game than the one we think is being played. The con artist is a phony playing a game of manipulation we are not "in" on. A game of poker may be a straightforward game of chance and skill to all the players, save one who is a cardsharp; a courtship may seem warmly romantic, unless one party is a gold digger or "lounge lizard" on the make for money or sex; the charismatic preacher may thrill his congregation with sermonic ardor until it is discovered he has absconded with the church funds. The con artist is controlling us even though we don't know it; by the time we find out we are the mark and the deal was phony, it may be too late to undo the flimflam. We discover that we thought we were playing, but rather were played with ("I've been had").

For most of us, the enchanted time of in-play contrasts with and is preferable to the earnest time of out-of-play and in-effort. Play is enchanting because it has a magical quality in which we become part of aesthetic and expressive activity. Whereas the earnest world of effort is unenchanted and often disenchanting, the alternative "unreal" world of illusionary play in the magic circle of *homo ludens* offers us entry into make-believe. One only has to observe schoolchildren to witness the contrast and preference. Time spent in class doing class*work* and speaking the language of school*work* and doing the chores of lab*work* is earnest effort designed (from the point of view of school) to educate children into becoming responsible and useful adults; from the point of view of the students, much of it is boring and painful, and school itself a confining prison. Witness when these same children are released during the playtime of recess. Their spirits soar, they run and frolic gaily, they engage in vigorous games and pretense, they are happy and enchanted, they exercise by having fun. When recess ends, the inmates are returned to their cells, their fun over except for the sweet memories, and they return with reluctance to their earnest duties as students. Why, they may ask, cannot all school, indeed all of life, be one big recess? Alas, these children in their simplicity do not understand that school, and much of adult social order, is designed to control the spirit and conduct of play.

PLAY AND SOCIETY: OR IS IT OK TO PLAY NOW?

One of the primary lessons we learn from social authorities such as parents and teachers and peers is that there is a time and place appropriate for certain things and inappropriate for others. "Society" tells us that one does not talk in church, throw chalk in class, or say gross or vulgar words at the dinner table. Church, school, and family gatherings call for appropriate behavior: one puts on the air of piety, attempts to pay sober attention to the teacher, sits up straight, and is "seen, not heard" at the dinner table. The "no-no" culture of socialization tells you what behavior is expected, and when, how, and why, and visits sanctions on you when you don't do the right thing. Knowing the right demeanor includes knowing when play in all its form is permitted and when it is not.

Let us consider the joke. "Joking around" can get you into trouble if you are giggling in church when another child makes faces, or passing notes in class, or say a "bad word" at the dinner table. Saying something funny—a wisecrack, making fun of someone, joshing with people, telling a "dirty" joke—can be embarrassing or even dangerous if told to the wrong people at the wrong time and in the wrong way. Readers familiar with the atmosphere on college campuses in the late twentieth century know about the "joke police." If you told a racist or sexist or whatever joke, however mild or, heaven forbid, funny, that "offended" someone, you could be brought up on charges and punished by campus authorities keen to enforce what came to be known as "political correctness." In fact, though, correctness in thought and action is and always has been a widespread expectation by social authorities. Only in the academic bastions of "free thought" did the surveillances of the thought police become ludicrous to the point of becoming, well, a joke. At the highest reaches of school, it turned out, the demand for orthodoxy in thought and action was no less than it was in, say, a rural Christian school or communist state school.

The point is that social authorities often frown on activities that are "all in fun" or in some sense playful. In the wrong context, play is not appropriate; therefore, the effort by institutions is to demarcate the right times and places for play, to control the definition of good and bad play and what play means. You are not as free to choose play as you might wish, and there are sociological reasons for that. If it is in the interest of social institutions to get you to think good thoughts and do good actions, then play can become a threatening "antisocial" form of behavior. Unwatched and unregulated play at recess can become a source of rebellion against the authority of school. The fear of anarchy—of bad thoughts and bad actions leading to rebellion—lurks in the heart of every institution. This fear includes the fear of fun "getting out of hand." The socio-logic of order excludes or tames the vital energy of play.

But why would something as seemingly harmless as children's play be such a threat? Because play left to itself teaches the wrong attitude. School is saying: "Life is not play." Life is real and life is earnest, and you have to keep your nose to the grindstone, feet on the ground, shoulder to the wheel, mind on your studies, and whatever other cliché that reminds you of the importance of school as serious business. In that social context, play is a privilege, a granted adjunct, a subsidiary activity. And play is something that school allows, directs, and takes away if deemed necessary. What was worse punishment than the loss of recess privileges?

The first social institutions we encounter, then, inform us that they are going to tell us when and how and why we will be permitted to play. In our free time as children, play was voluntary, and usually our primary activity. Play was central to our "life order," since they

were those activities we chose to do. In play, we learned how to nego-
tiate rules and situations ("Let's play this way"), the settings of play
("Let's play here"), and the time of play ("Let's play for a while"). But
like family obligations, school is not voluntary and chosen. Rather it
is something to which we were *sent*. School is part of the institutional
order, those activities we are told we have to do. Thus the activities of
school are not so much negotiated as they are imposed—not "Let's
play" but rather, "You will do as we say." In school, playtime is controlled by the authorities, and the "play attitude" is condemned and
the "earnest attitude" praised. You will behave this way, in this
place, at this time. Since social institutions demand that we take
them seriously, the introduction of play in the wrong context becomes a potential source of subversion. Playing around in class signals that we are not taking the teacher, and by extension school,
seriously enough, so we will have to be corrected in our attitude (or at
least in our outward demeanor: we may still hate school, but appear
as if we're taking algebra and ancient history seriously when in fact
we're daydreaming). The appearance of earnestness becomes the
norm, and we learn the social role expected by the institution.

We also learn that institutional authorities control the time, place,
and conduct of play. At recess, we are told, "You will now play." But not
just any play that we may choose. Violent play is controlled and punished, and often recess consists of structured play: "You will now play
this game by these rules and we will supervise." And also when it
ends: "Recess is over, children. Return to class." Indeed, as we grow
older, we learn that school takes play seriously and expects an earnest attitude from athletes. The games sponsored by school are not
the occasion for mere fun: too much is at stake—reputation, school
loyalty, the social ethic of winning. Thus the message of organized
school sports is often not "Have fun" but rather, "You will win." The intrinsic meaning of play—having fun—is superceded by an extrinsic
meaning: winning is important to school. Even the many of us who
watch the few play are expected to enjoy the game in a certain way
("You will ardently cheer for our side to urge them onward to victory"). Here play has become serious business. Very early on, even before school, the social conduct of play separates us into spectators
and participants. The physical play of early youth and adolescence
often means that those with size and dexterity become the participants, and the rest who are small, uncoordinated, and afraid become
the spectators. Later, mental dexterity and social skills become important in other forms of social play, such as chess, music, conversation, and sexual courtship.

Long ago the great German sociologist Georg Simmel wrote about the "play-forms of society."[15] He was interested in all those ways that we create contexts of play that are relatively autonomous, that is, freed from the earnest restraints and purposes of institutions such as school. Autonomous play occurs in artificial worlds of "sociability," wherein we engage in more informal social games such as conversation and coquetry, or flirting. Conversation at a dinner party can be great fun in a variety of ways—storytelling, joshing and joking, social "one-upmanship," intellectual games, drunken condemnations of the sorry state of the world, expressions of smug self-satisfaction, fond remembrances of things past, and so on. Flirting is a social game fraught with both delicious anticipation and dangerous liaisons. In both instances, the play form is in a sense "play in itself" in that no action is required nor purpose defined. Here informal play is just what it is, conversing or flirting or whatever for the pure hell of it. To be sure, sometimes a dinner party or episode of flirting can lead to something else, such as a solicitation of charity funds or a love affair or sexual harassment suit. But then, like school sports, the event has taken on an earnest meaning beyond having fun and then forgetting it. Play-in-itself is an episode of playing around without involvement or extrinsic purpose. The catharsis of conversation was satisfying, but the dinner party wrote no manifestos and lynched no miscreants. The flirtatious couple only flirted, and no passionate encore ensued. The play was enough, and called for no subsequent action. Play-forms at their best may be just play and nothing more, in the autonomous and momentary spirit of, "The hell with it. Let's play."

THE VAST PLAYGROUND OF MYTH, AND THE EQUALLY VAST MYTH OF THE PLAYGROUND

We can usefully think of play as occurring in social recesses, places, and times designated for play. Play can range from the anarchic to the informal to the formal. Play can be a delightful autonomous respite from the world of earnest endeavor, or it can be organized into something that has a social purpose beyond the fun of it. In any case, a social recess allows for a change in, and often a suspension of, social rules. This is why we so often think of play as an interlude, intermission, intermezzo, pause, interim, interval, rest, break, seclusion, retreat, repose, and respite. Playtime is different, and we come to it hoping that it will satisfy our desire for play. We think it "natural" to want to play, and our society deems it good for us to play some to "re-create" ourselves for our normal social duties.

Even though not everyone, nor every society, values play, there is by now a vast mythic heritage that gives play its exalted and special status in our hierarchy of values.

To begin at the *very* beginning, there is the myth that humankind began in a "state of play," or lived in a prelapsarian Edenic state in which people devoted themselves largely to play. In the Eden of Judeo-Christian tradition, Adam and Eve lived in a state of perpetual innocence, because they had not eaten the fruit of the tree of knowledge of good and evil. The state of childish play in the Garden is ended when they yield to temptation and are expelled from Eden, with woman condemned to painful childbirth and sex as original sin, and the man condemned to painful work, living and eating by the sweat of his brow. This powerful myth includes the idea that somehow our original state was one of relaxed and bountiful play, which we either will return to in heaven or should try to recapture here on Earth.

The manifestations of the myth of "original play" take many forms. It has been transferred to scientific efforts to reconstruct the evolution of species. Consider this *Time-Life* portrayal of the daily life of Australopithecines, one of our proto-human ancestors: they had "a great deal of leisure time," and "their needs [were] few and easily met in a warm, benign environment. When there is enough to eat throughout the year, there is little else to do but sit around." This "abundance of free time" led to "socializing" (such as "spry youngsters chase one another around an acacia tree on the African savanna"), "the period of infancy, childhood and adolescence became longer and longer," and most days were a "relaxed day." Sounds pretty nice—"Edenic" even. But alas, this idyllic life, some think, ended with the growth of intelligence, of civilization, and of social hierarchy and discipline, such as the advent of school with the Sumerians. There is even a novel called *The Inheritors* by Nobel laureate William Golding, which speculates that Neanderthal man was still living in a state of play—innocent, happy, playful—in the Neolithic age, but was superceded by a new version of human, Cro-Magnon man, who was smart, cunning, driven, and earnest—namely, us.[16]

It was the philosopher Rousseau who gave modern impetus to the myth of natural man and the worship of nature. The idea that we are born free and are everywhere in chains gave new force to the myth of the Fall, but it is from nature we have fallen, and civilization is the hindrance. If we were to return to our original play-life state, we would recover our lost true state. Some of the same mythic yearnings inform environmentalists today: if we could recover the sacred grove of an ecological paradise, we would again frolic in a natural world devoid of the satans of pollution and development, and humanity would be freed from the drives of greed and exploitation that foul the human nest. The myth of "natural humanity" persists in our romantic belief in the innocence and wisdom of children, peasants, and poets, whose intimacy with nature imbues them with natural virtue, and thus the ability to have fun, frolic gaily, and be happy.

The myth of Eden in its various forms remains a powerful vision, the chimera that in some original state we were creatures of pure play, and that we could or should return to that innocent and free condition under the right circumstances. For some psychologists, such visions seem suspiciously like yearnings for a pre-adult state of childish fun, the "age regression" to childish irresponsibility, or searching for the "inner child." Our imaginings that "precivilized" people such as Adam and Eve or the Australopithecines spent their days in an eternal summer of lazy funning may be a psychic impulse to imagine what many adults (not to mention students) desire: escape from the grind of work, the sobriety of the earnest attitude, and the boredom of habit and "the reality principle." The alternative "pleasure principle" lurks in the libidinal energy latent in our id, expressed in fantasies of Edenic escapes to sexual fulfillment. In our wildest fantasies, we would like to make all time into playtime. It was no less than Dr. Freud, in his book *Civilization and Its Discontents*, who thought that the instinctive desires of humankind to exercise "the pleasure principle" in sexual and other satisfying play were irredeemably at odds with the orderly and earnest requirements of civilization. Thus the individual had to be civilized into relinquishing the basic instinctive desire to minimize pain and maximize pleasure, giving up the natural state of play for the psychic and social discipline (repression into earnestness) necessary for civilization. Here we expel ourselves from Eden.[17]

But if many of the social and historical analysts of play are correct, playtime occurs in a culture, and indeed is *essential* to the continuity and nature of culture. Many of any society's cultural forms—games, stagecraft, toys, rituals and liturgies, music, folklore, and so on—originated in play, and over time came to be not merely playful but rather essential to the conduct of cultural life. It is in a cultural context that play comes to be a *habit*, something that we anticipate and conduct as a regular and repeated feature of social life. Play becomes part of the rhythm of the day and the calendar. In this way, play is cultured, so that social authorities can say, "This is playtime" and, "This is not playtime." School decides when recess begins and ends, and what play is appropriate during recess; when it ends, the earnest conduct of schoolwork begins anew. In this balanced view, we need both earnestness and playfulness, work and leisure, to fulfill ourselves. All play and no work makes Jacks and Jills just as dull as the opposite.

Nevertheless, our mythic imaginings of the origins of play belie a belief that before the advent of social order and habit and authoritative rules, there was a world of people capable of play, which civilized life controlled and suppressed. We may expect that things were not that simple. Indeed, one quite respectable school of thought even says that civilization—people settling down in permanent towns and cities—may have originated in play, or more accurately, in the discovery of a well-known instrument of play: beer. Around ten thousand years or so ago, people in the "fertile crescent" of the Near East were still largely wandering hunters and gatherers. What motivated them to settle down and go to all the trouble of sowing, cultivating, and reaping crops? The hypothesis is that at some point someone accidentally discovered that wild wheat and barley, left in the open, did not spoil but that natural yeast in the air converted it into a bubbling brew that made those who drank it feel good. The incentive to stay in one place and raise crops was now great: the loss of mobility and the work involved was thought worth it to produce a drink that brought about temporary euphoria and relaxation. Indeed, in these early settlements, individuals and groups appeared to have invested great effort and even risk to produce sufficient quantities of beer. Beer eventually broke these Neolithic peoples' ties to hunting and gathering, even though that way of life was less onerous, chancy, and even more reliable as a source of food. In many of these early agricultural cultures, beer was elevated to a high status in social and religious practice, and by the time of Sumeria, about five thousand years ago, beer was central to social life, to the extent that any disruption in the supply constituted a serious breach of habit and diet (beer was second only to animal protein as a human nutrient).[18] This theory is likely too simple, too, but it has a degree of mythic plausibility to anyone who has frequented a British pub or a German beer garden.

What we do not fully understand about these early societies is how they integrated beer drinking into the rhythms and habits of life. But what is of interest here is that a "mind-altering" food—perhaps the first that humankind had discovered—may have been considered so important that it altered a previously established and even "superior" way of life. Drinking beer was a source of playfulness, diminishing pain and lowering inhibitions in that familiar alcoholic glow. The euphoria produced was elevated to a religious experience of some significance, since it apparently was felt that the "divine madness" of getting high and feeling good was an unusual psychic and physical state and thus must be a gift from, and a way to commune with, the gods. If there is merit in this theory of origins, Dr. Freud was slightly mistaken: perhaps the founders of civilizations tended to give up the freedom of wandering for the settled regularity of play. (In that tradition, those who overimbibe at a party can rationalize such excess as participation in ancient ritual practice.)

By the time of the Greeks, the Dionysian (Roman Bacchus) cults had made first beer drinking and then wine drinking into a sacred cult, including rites in which thoroughly respectable women would leave home for sacred woods in the hills to participate in ecstatic ceremonies that celebrated the god of wine. These orgiastic rites included tearing animals to pieces and eating them raw, and killing any uninvited man who happened by. Even though this kind of ritual play was in a religious context and setting, the message of "It's funtime" was part of the event, producing *enthusias*, or "enthusiasm" for a spiritual, and apparently also physical, orgy. The term "bacchanal" refers to the sacralized funtime of Greek women (to capture the spirit of such a mythic playtime, read Euripides' play *Bacchae* while listening to Stravinsky's *The Rite of Spring*).

We are used to sacral time being organized as somewhat more piously holy, or at least decorous. But such religious enthusiasm survives in evangelical and fervent branches of religion, such as Pentecostal Christianity and Shiite Islam. These ancient practices remind us that funtime can occur in a variety of cultural recesses. A "religious orgy" seems to us a contradiction in terms, but different times and places define what fun is and when funtime can happen in an astounding variety of ways. "This is recess; go out and play" can and has been observed in politics, business, agriculture, family life, you name it. Perhaps one of the most familiar forms of peripety, or rites of role reversal, that permits a temporary recess in the hierarchy and roles of society is the Saturnalia. Many societies throughout history have found a place for such a playtime, wherein commoners can mock or insult their king or even play at being him, women can deride or mimic men, resentments can be voiced without fear of reprisal, and so on. Such rituals can include free expression of lewd or obscene talk, theft, sexual license, and even doing everything backward (as with the famous Contrary Warriors of the Cheyenne Indians). The Roman "feast of fools" was common in Europe until the modern age, and the spirit of Saturnalia survives in such extant playtimes as Halloween, New Year's Eve, Mardi Gras, and demolition derbies.

Not everybody likes merriment and revelry and social mockery or for that matter, playtime in general. At various places and times, civilizations have gone to great lengths to restrict play, promote seriosity, and repress the pleasure principle. But for causes and reasons we will elaborate below, the development of civilization has reached a stage at which it is quite possible that the exercise of play will expand dramatically. It is our argument that we are entering a new phase of history characterized so much by play that we can deem it a *play world*. The myth of play has retained its powerful grip on our imagination to the extent that many of us now believe that myth can become reality, the pleasure principle can be incorporated into civilization, and the Dionysian expression of joy and even ecstasy is not a threat but a promise. We are moving from a world ruled by heavy gods to a world that sports light gods. Heavy gods ruled us by the threat of sanction, but the new gods of lightness beckon us with the promise of happiness and joy. How we got to this moment of hope is our subject.

AIN'T WE GOT FUN?

The astute reader, herself or himself playing with the text, has grasped the obvious. The author has tried to invite interest in play by treating the concept of play as an existential possibility, as a sociological form, and as a mythic inheritance now translating into a temporal process. Play is the act of having fun, play is the social form of funning, and the myth of play begets cumulative fun over time. We discussed play in a playfully diffident manner: it is slippery, but as the judge said of obscenity, we know it when we see it. We also thought that play is something that social orders recognize as important, and like freedom, often try hard to control or ration. And we observed that throughout history, different times and places have accorded various importance to, and toleration of, play. This lets us see play separately and together as a individual activity, as a social activity, and as a historical activity often accorded mythic status. Throughout the book, we will combine our study of play with these three dimensions—play as an analytical concept, as a social form, and as temporal process.

These dimensions suggest three theses about play that we will argue for subsequently:

1. For a variety of historical and social reasons, our personal ability to, willingness for, and expectation of play has increased exponentially in recent times. We have developed knowledge of play, see the value of play, and wish for the joy of play. Our *attitude* toward play is changing. As never before, we *want* to play.

2. Concomitantly, modern societies increasingly allow and provide the social opportunity and cultural legitimacy of play. In contemporary societies, play has acquired an indispensable quality, and the ability of societies to define, demarcate, and channel play has diminished. Thus the time, energy, and wealth devoted to play has increased, with widespread social consequences. The *social opportunity* for play is becoming available for large populations. Society offers more people than ever the *chance* to play.

3. Looking forward, we may anticipate that as the variety and dimensions of play expand, this new social condition will create an unprecedented world of play and players. The world of the future, we predict, will be increasingly organized around the mythic hope and social principle of play. In the early decades of the twenty-first century "postmodernity," the fundamental existential hope, social fact, and expanding activity will be play. Our posterity will witness the coming preponderance of play, and will engage in an unprecedented *pursuit of happiness* defined as the ability to have fun. The future may well involve the political assertion of the *right* to play.

To explore these theses, our inquiry into play will be divided into three distinct modes: the *dynamics* of play, the *pragmatics* of play, and the *futuristics* of play. The first chapter deals with the developmental analysis of history with the emergence of play as central to the social processes leading to the present. This initial discussion deals with the development of the *economy* of play, focusing on those economic innovations that have given impetus to behavioral habits of play; the development of the *culture* of play, in particular those cultural innovations that encourage the spread of the *ethos* of play; and the development of playful *politics*, the ways in which the political world became increasingly playful, and how this has changed the conduct of politics and indeed the expanse of the play world. Throughout, we will attempt to envision the process of playing as dynamic, highlighting those historical innovations and practices that have given impetus to the creation of the play world.

Chapter 2 will examine the *pragmatics* of play, the contemporary ways in which the principle and practice of play are being utilized. If we are correct to think that the temporal dynamics of play are creating a new ludenic order, then how this propensity for play is being organized and utilized is important to know. In turn, we will discuss how we are witnessing the creation of a world leisure class, with a multiplicity of play options and connections (and we will also reveal how you might join it!). The universal lure of play, we will further argue, is being enhanced by the global reach and alluring messages of play emanating from the world media. Further, we will build on these discussions to note that the spread of leisure classes and media connections is now redefining the context of politics as an activity conducted as play and enhancing the ability to play.

Chapter 3 will conclude by looking forward to the future of play. This involves the tricky art of intelligent speculation about the role of play in the world of tomorrow. (Many of the younger readers of this book will live well into the twenty-first century.) But since the expansion of play and the ludenic "pursuit of happiness" is a distinct and significant historical possibility, it behooves us to regard such a development as likely to make the future different from the present. So we will examine the consequences, intended and unintended, of a future play economy that expands the current "entertainment economy" into a social principle. The cultural corollary of a future social order based in play deserves forecasting. What would a "play culture" be like, and what does a culture of play produce?

After these last paragraphs, the reader may have that will-this-be-on-the-exam? feeling. After playing around with play, the suspicion might be that now we are going to abandon our playful attitude and get down to the work of play. We fondly hope we don't kill the spirit of play as we proceed on our inquiry. We can be inquisitive without being stuffy, curious without being pedantic, and interested without being boring. It may be that the joy of play for adults is that it combines both youthful enthusiasm and mature reflection in acts of enjoyment. Reading a book should be no less an act of enjoyment, especially when it is a book about people having fun. The musement of play is nonetheless play. So let us play the muse.

NOTES

1. Mihaly Csikszentmihalyi and Stith Bennett, "An Exploratory Model of Play," *American Anthropologist*, 73, no. 1 (February 1971): 45–58.

2. Walter Kaufmann, ed., "From the Gay Science," in *The Portable Nietzsche* (New York: Viking Press, 1954), pp. 93–101.

3. Charles Sanders Peirce, quoted in Umberto Eco and Thomas A. Sebeok, *The Sign of Three* (Bloomington: Indiana University Press, 1983), p. 195.

4. See David Cohen, *The Development of Play* (Washington Square, NY: New York University Press, 1987); D. E. Berlyne, "Laughter, Humor, and Play," *The Handbook of Social Psychology*, ed. Gardner Lindzey and Elliot Aronson, 2d ed., vol. 3 (Reading, MA: Addison-Wesley, 1970), pp. 795–852; Vivian Paley, *Bad Guys Don't Have Birthdays: Fantasy Play at Four* (Chicago: University of Chicago Press, 1987).

5. Gregory Bateson, "A Theory of Play and Fantasy," *Psychiatric Research Reports* 2 (1955): 39–51.

6. William Stephenson, *The Play Theory of Mass Communication* (Chicago: University of Chicago Press, 1967), p. 60.

7. Johan Huizinga, *Homo Ludens: A Study of the Play Element in Culture* (Boston: Beacon Press, 1955), pp. 1, 3.

8. Ibid., p. 8.

9. Csikszentimihalyi and Bennett, "Exploratory Model," p. 45.

10. Clifford Geertz, "Deep Play: Notes on the Balinese Cockfight," in *The Interpretation of Cultures* (New York: Basic Books, 1973), pp. 412–453.

11. James E. Combs and Michael Mansfield, eds., *Drama in Life: The Uses of Communication in Society* (New York: Hastings House, 1976); Theodor H. Gaster, *Thespis* (New York: Norton, 1977).

12. Manfred Wolf, "It's, Like, Speech Becomes a Performance," *Des Moines Register*, August 25, 1995, p. 9R; Ruth Finnegan, *Oral Poetry* (Cambridge: Cambridge University Press, 1977).

13. Catherine Garvey, *Play* (Cambridge: Harvard University Press, 1977), pp. 4–7.

14. Erving Goffmann, *Frame Analysis* (New York: Harper & Row, 1974).

15. Georg Simmel, *The Sociology of Georg Simmel*, trans. and ed. by Kurt H. Wolff (New York: Free Press of Glencoe, 1964), pp. 43–44.

16. William Golding, *The Inheritors* (New York: Harcourt Brace Harvest Books, 1963); Maitland A. Edey and the editors of Time-Life Books, *The Emergence of Man: The Missing Link* (New York: Time-Life Books, 1972), pp. 28–29.

17. Sigmund Freud, *Civilization and Its Discontents* (New York: Norton, 1962).

18. William K. Stevens, "Fabric of Civilization Traced to Beer," *Chicago Tribune*, April 25, 1985, Tempo section, p. 4.

CHAPTER 1

The Dynamics of Play

Since we all live in time, have a past, and know that before we lived there were pasts, we quite naturally are curious about the past, and how it has shaped the world into what it is today. As the philosopher Wittgenstein asked, When the present becomes the past, where does it go? Well, one answer is that it doesn't go away; the past is not dead, because it is not even past. Rather the past remains in the present through the *dynamic* of historical change. In any present, we *use* the past to understand the persisting patterns that shape the time in which we live. *Dynamis* in Greek suggested power and ability; understanding history requires comprehension of the dynamics of innovation, often with consequences both unintended and far reaching. The dynamic question here is, How did we acquire from the past the power and the ability to play?

One distinguished political scientist, Harold D. Lasswell, thought we should think of social dynamics in terms of "developmental analysis." History is not a matter of establishing a sequence of events, such as dates or dynasties; nor is it clearly a series of occurrences happening in a cycle or a set of progressive stages. But the temporal processes of social history are also not random or inconsequential. Lasswell thought we should think of society as a "continuum of social change" and social power as a "process in time." Thus inquiry should be guided by "the principle of temporality" and a vision of what's happening as "patterns of successions of events." In so doing, we come to understand not only what people have done and are doing, but also what can or might be done in the future to anticipate or guide developments. Knowledge of the dynamics of social temporality leads to pragmatic evaluation and action in order to cope with change.[1]

A tall order, but not insurmountable. Inquirers just have to make informed judgments as to what happened that is important to know, and how what happened affects what is happening and what might happen. Understanding the dynamics of human processes ultimately involves the *play of creative imagination*, making for ourselves metaphorical pictures or images of what has gone on and the relationship of that to what is going on. Ultimately our explanation of human developments, past and present, comes down to what seems sensible to say about what people did and are doing. In other words, which explanation can you do the most with? Which one can you really play with, conjure with, "run" with?

Take what is at the core of developmental analysis: explaining innovation. Why do things change, and new things enter the world? People really do live in the immediate present, and do what they think is the thing to do at the time. But for complex or even odd reasons, they sometimes manage to do things that bring about innovations and consequences far beyond what they may have intended or dreamed. Specifically here, in the course of modern history it was very serious people with quite earnest attitudes and solemn purposes who, ironically, created the expanding world of play. People who wished to return to a simple faith or reactivated past state of virtue became the unwitting authors of secular society with all its trimmings. What is worth knowing in developmental analysis are consequences; thus we focus less on the "cause of things" and more on the *things caused*, in this case, the play world. How did we get to the temporal point so that now people are playing more?

FROM MAX WEBER

The great German sociologist Max Weber (1864–1920), in about 1905 conceived a famous developmental construct that is relevant to our subject here. He was generally interested in how social and economic change occurs. Specifically, he studied the historical rise of capitalism in Europe and America. How, he asked, did the ideology of modern capitalism triumph over time against law, custom, institutions that opposed such activities as usury (lending money at interest), powerful social groups such as landed aristocracies, and institutions such as the church? It did so, Weber thought, by the blending in Protestant, especially Puritan, thought and attitudes, of the holy and the earthly. The "deadly sin" of greed and avarice had always existed, but in the early modern period economic gain was legitimated by the religious as a sacred duty. Capitalism triumphed, especially in Protestant countries such as Holland and England, because it now had a moral basis. The ascetic Protestants thought that a secular "calling" or "vocation" was a legitimate activity, and that indeed, success in your vocation may well be a sign of your Christian virtue (work, sobriety, punctuality, frugality, indeed all the virtues useful for business success) and even of your status as a member of the elect to be saved. In this way of thinking, building a business enterprise and making (and saving) lots of money was an outward and visible sign of an inward and spiritual grace. The Puritans were not worshipers of success, since that was the sin of pride, but they were interested in promoting secular piety through the cultivation of earnest attitudes and habits, precisely those that made a vocation into worldly success. A calling could now be pursued with the sanctity of religious responsibility, and the acquisition of riches, once thought inimical to piety, was now welcomed as God's providential reward for the pious doing their duty to increase their estate, and furthering the Kingdom of God.

Earnest diligence at one's worldly tasks becomes a moral duty, and quite unintentionally gives enormous credence to those attitudes and practices that characterize the capitalist world. The stern collectivism and punitive nature of Calvin's Geneva or Puritan New England foresaw no rampant individualism, orgy of materialism, or worship of Mammon. Nevertheless, the descendants of the Puritan spiritual revolutionaries have become instead economic revolutionaries, helping to make the modern world into one that is increasingly secular, acquisitive, and hedonistic! If Weber is correct, it is a supreme historical irony that those earnest Christians who tried to make a more religious world in effect were instrumental in creating a world where the "spirit" of capitalism became the secular religion. The religious ascetic who exercises his or her faith and hope (alleviating what Weber called "salvation anxiety") through diligent labor at a vocation is eventually superceded by economic ascetics who exercise their faith and hope in profit and accumulation through diligent labor at a vocation, alleviating what we might call "gain anxiety."[2]

Weber's thesis has been much disputed, but to most analysts there is a kernel of truth in this reconstruction of change from the medieval to the modern world. Note that the earnest attitude and serious demeanor of the Puritan was expressed most adequately at the level of everyday life and pursuits through *work*. Puritan sermons are full of praise for those who toil, since that self-denying activity is godly, but time wasting, idleness, impure thoughts, pleasure seeking, and sensual pursuits are ungodly. Eventually, these habits meant that work had both a theological foundation as a moral duty and a rational foundation as the methodical way to utilize time and effort that produced goods and services. Thus the innovations of science and technology that made work more "rational" were welcomed, and imposing the discipline of the "work ethic" on schoolchildren and industrial workers and household staffs and peasants became better organized. The historical result of this change was the creation of modern organizations—the state, the corporation, the school—all based on the premise that organized and directed work is an "economy of effort" that leads to fruitful results.

Recall that in school one of the first "metalessons" we learn is that "work pays off." We were told that if you could learn how to delay gratification, use your time well, adapt an attitude of earnest concentration, pay attention in class, attend regularly and punctually, do your lessons well and on schedule—in other words if we *worked hard*—we would succeed at school, and by dint of our work habits would therefore likely succeed at life. Indeed, the more schooling we got, the more likely we were to acquire knowledge and skills that would mean success in business, law, medicine, or whatever vocation we chose. We were constantly reminded of the importance of being earnest.

School's essential task, then, was to teach us not so much how or even what to think, but rather how to work. The work ethic became central to the moral teachings of school, and even though it was rooted in the moral philosophy of Puritanism, it was gradually transferred to the moral philosophy of capitalism. Even children's stories such as "The Little Engine That Could" were parables in which the moral to the story was the satisfaction of sustained effort ("I think I can, I think I can . . .") leading to ensured success ("I knew I could, I knew I could . . ."). As school expanded into "universal education," it ceased to become a place where scholars pondered the big questions and became instead an organization that taught us how to behave properly in organizational life and how to think properly about work, and acted as a workplace that prepared us for the workplace. We emerged from school believing that work gave one dignity, that sloth and laziness lead to misery and poverty, and that those who suc-

ceeded the most and the least at work were both justly rewarded.
(The Puritans who ruled in seventeenth-century England opposed
alms for the poor, since giving relief to the wickedly idle would be a
sin, supporting through charity drunkenness and gluttony. Such
fears are the direct ancestor of Ronald Reagan's apocryphal tales of
"welfare queens" who support a Cadillac on welfare checks and people who buy steaks and vodka with food stamps.)

The eminent philosopher Hannah Arendt sees productive labor as
an essential element of "the human condition," the form of activity
that produces the "human artifact."[3] But envisioning humankind as
homo faber—people as makers and workers—is fraught with the difficulty that Weber (and others, such as Karl Marx and Werner Sombart) understood. The way that labor has come to be organized and
rewarded in the modern world is historically specific, as organized
and directed labor we think of as *work*—jobs, tasks, toil, employment, occupation, the daily grind. The attitudes and behaviors that
have made for "the work world" are not universal. Not every time and
place and group have valued or conducted work in the same way, nor
is it necessarily "natural" for people to work, and want to work, in the
same way and at the same pace that the modern world has deemed
valuable and correct. When we say, "Everyone should work" or
"Those who will not work should not eat," we are articulating a social
attitude gestated in the early modern period. And such aphorisms
sound suspiciously like the "official" philosophy of societies committed to work, and those elites—the people who run things—who benefit the most from work. The rhetoric of the joy, dignity, and pleasure of
work—*laborare est orare*—is often an exhortation by a boss—a principal, a corporate CEO, or a politician—to inspire us to work all the
harder and longer for them.

The modern world of work came from somewhere, and much of
that "somewhere" remains in Puritan-based attitudes and expectations that are still passed on and affect the conduct of society (especially in the United States). But the "somewhere it went" did not turn
out quite the way the early Puritans, and for that matter the early
capitalists, thought it would. The earnest Puritan attitude that valued work underwrote and overcame impediments to the spread of organized work in the economic and organizational revolution that
developed modernity as we now know it, a long way from Calvin's Geneva or Winthrop's Plymouth. The Puritan attitude of earnestness
was at first strange to the world of medieval arrangements such as
privileged leisure and cavalier habits of sloth and pleasurable excess. Eventually, that strangeness became familiar at the historical

point where religious discipline converged with emerging economic interests in a new dynamic of innovation. This unity of sacral piety and profane enterprise made for the creation of a *moral economy*, giving normative sanction for the organization of effort and realization of gain. As we shall see, what is now becoming strange is the persistence of the Puritanical rhetoric of severity and pain and the "late modern" reality of a desacralized world offering plenty and pleasure. Perhaps in some impish way, history is now defeating the Puritans and allowing the Cavaliers the final triumph!

EMINENT VICTORIANS

Weber saw England as one of the historical foci of the rise of modern society. By the nineteenth century, the new forms of modern organization were in their inception in England as well as other parts of Europe. In England, we begin to see the dynamic of the moral economy, in the social consequences of the new capitalist gift for innovation and organization, and also the human consequences of the demand for increased worker productivity through labor discipline. Perhaps most importantly, by now we see the development of the secular entrepreneurial attitude that takes precedence over and provides explanatory power for all social relations. Everything becomes subordinate to and functional for productive and profitable work. This is what the greatest student of capitalism, Werner Sombart, meant when he wrote of the "absolutism" of the acquisition principle: "[A] human being is regarded merely as labor power, nature as an instrument of production, life as one grand commercial transaction, heaven and earth as a large business concern in which everything that lives and moves is registered in a gigantic ledger in terms of its money value."[4] The unity of religious sanction and economic innovation was now complete. The morality of the economy allowed the mobilization of everyone to be busy working for a busy-ness.

In the early Industrial Revolution, the new religion of capitalism quickly mobilized peasant and artisan labor into what William Blake called "the dark satanic mills" wherein, according to William Wordsworth, every value "is offered up/To Gain, the master idol of the realm, Perpetual sacrifice." The new mills used advances in machine technology, such as the spinning jenny, to make more efficient the production of goods such as woolens. Craft labor was superceded by "rationalized" work. Apologists then and now have maintained that the new working schedule for workers actually improved their lives from their previous existence. But the brutal hours (including those of young children), starvation wages, frequent accidents, and hovels in which they slept the few hours allowed them hardly sound like an improvement over much of anything.

Indeed, in the peasant and artisan culture immediately preceding the factory system, at least there was some sense of the rhythms of the seasons, respite from labor during the lax winter months, a feeling of place and permanence, and the relaxed pace of village life. Artisans in particular, such as croppers or shearers, cotton weavers, and framework knitters, used traditional craft technologies to ply their trade among villagers. But the new factories could produce cottons and stockings more efficiently, quickly threatening to dispossess these local artisans. In response, many of these workmen formed into a virtual insurrectionist group known to history as the Luddites (after a mythical General Ludd, who led them in their nighttime raids and signed their letters of intimidation). The Luddites destroyed machinery, burned factories, frightened budding industrialists, and even killed, resulting in British regular troops being sent—without much result since the local rebels enjoyed popular support and protection—into hotbeds of Luddism such as Nottinghamshire (the home of Robin Hood!). The Luddite revolt was finally suppressed, but the active resistance became part of the folklore of the long struggle to organize the English working class.[5]

The example of the Luddite revolt serves to remind us that those who were utilized, and in many cases victimized, by the Industrial Revolution were not happy with what was happening to them and their way of life. The new precision labor discipline imposed on them in the new factories made for dreary and painful work that rewarded them little, and if they were injured or somehow lax, they were thrown away. People in regions of Luddite strength had memories of relatively relaxed days working in fields or craft shops in villages, and also memories of *folk play*. The rural rhythm of life included many periods of play such as "holy days," weddings and feasts, and seasonal festivities. The Puritans had frowned upon such playful and joyous occasions, and indeed attempted to ban Christmas with its pagan origins in Yule logs and mistletoe and partying, wedding feasts, and ancient festive activities such as morris dancing. But by this later time, the "religion of gain" had superceded the holy Puritans, and the new entrepreneurs attempted to instill the earnest attitude and habits of work in this brand new proletariat, destroying much of folk play by revolutionizing daily habits and monopolizing time. So what was lost was free time, relaxed time, and festive time:

these were the first modern people to lose their habits of play to the imposed requirements of work. Children as young as four worked in the new mills, and they essentially had no childhood. The familial and social bonds of the cottage industries were replaced by the rigid timetable, restrictions, and punishments of industrial routine, including bans on the convivial tradition of talking, whistling, and singing while working. People no longer owned their labor; they also no longer owned their time. Work was organized by their employers, and so was time. The new industrial proletariat had their work and their day measured by the discipline of the machine and the clock.

Here we begin to see, then, the painful beginnings of the modern economy of work. In some measure we are all still descendants of the Puritans and the capitalist entrepreneurs of the Industrial Revolution, still carrying in our heads the beliefs that created modernity. But we are also aware of what was lost when these new attitudes and habits were realized in their full consequences. This is no more evident than in the writings of Charles Dickens, who saw what "heroic materialism" was for those who suffered under its discipline, or even those who benefited from it, and saw that both had lost something important: the opportunity, or even the ability, to play.

Dickens's novels and stories dramatize the consequences of the new world of labor's industrialization and what is euphemistically called "capital accumulation." As someone who had suffered as a child under the harsh conditions of early nineteenth-century England, he describes the grim new world by the institution that is to make the young into compliant and efficient workers—school—in his best novel on the subject, *Hard Times*. Dickens saw that the school was designed to reflect the mill, and was there not to educate to free the minds of the young but rather to train them to be compliant and useful workers. (One utilitarian system of education offered in Victorian England was called The Steam Engine of the Moral World.) Thomas Gradgrind, the teacher of working-class children in "Coketown" (Preston), wants them to learn nothing but "Facts. Facts alone are wanted in life. Plant nothing else, and root out everything else." Gradgrind remonstrates a little girl for engaging in "fancy." "You must discard the word Fancy altogether." Gradgrind's colleague, Mr. M'choakumchild, brags that he graduated from a teacher's college "factory" full of facts with which he is determined to fill the heads of students. In the new industrial ideology, schools were factories, teachers were executives, and students full of facts were the product, prepared to enter the work life of mill drudgery. Clearly such a prospect of schooling and working is grim indeed. The meta-

phor of the machine and the regimen of fact by this point almost totally excludes play. (One of Dickens's characters in *Hard Times*,
with a lisp, says, "People muthe be amuthed. They can't be alwayth a
learning, nor yet they can't be alwayth a working, they an't made for
it.") Indeed, there probably is no figure in literature more of an exem-
plary capitalist than Dickens's Ebenezer Scrooge. The Ghost of
Christmas Past shows Scrooge at an earlier age, whose face "had begun to wear the signs of care and avarice," with "an eager, greedy,
restless motion in the eye." His fiancée releases him from his vow because "another idol has replaced me . . . a golden one," and now his
"nobler aspirations fall off one by one, until the master-passion,
Gain, engrosses you." By adopting this attitude, Scrooge realizes the
ideal of weighing "everything by Gain," considers such frivolities as
Christmas to be "humbug," and refuses to contribute to charity because he already pays taxes for the poorhouse and treadmill and
prison.[6]

So the religion of gain was a solemn one indeed, and no less than
the earnest Puritanism of old saw threat in such "misconduct" as
singing on the job or children entertaining fancies. Gradgrind and
the mill masters are clear secular descendants of the Puritan spirit,
wherein organizations such as school and factory must be so ordered
as to exclude any ludenic behavior. The idea that "people must be
amused" and cannot be forced into virtually constant earnest effort
at school or work never occurs to them. The new prosperity was
bought by ruthless exploitation of organized laborious effort with
the price of poverty of spirit. For both the managers and the managed, experience narrowed.

But for others, experience expanded. Sociologist Robert Merton
has argued that Puritanism not only produced as an unanticipated
consequence the spirit and practice of capitalism, but inadvertently
created the spirit and practice of modern science. The early modern
scientists believed that God's laws could be understood as part of a
rational and orderly universe. By the time of early capitalism, science was not only legitimate as inquiry, it was also useful in the technology it created—the steam engine, the railroad, the industrial
machinery. But more broadly, such innovation in thought also gave
credence to a new attitude: scientific investigation. If the currents of
modern thought created capitalism and its critics from Luddites to
Marxists to trade unions, it also created science and its critics.[7]

But the spirit of scientific investigation had the ironic effect of
challenging conventional wisdom through discovery by using freedom of thought. Out of this came *scientific play*, the spirit of inquiry

that investigates things once thought unfathomable and solves mysteries once thought unsolvable. This spirit of "what if . . . ?" led to Darwin and Freud and Max Weber and Einstein. But it also led to Sherlock Holmes. The fictional Holmes exemplifies the spirit of scientific play, using evidence and logic to solve mysteries. Holmes is depicted as a paragon of rationality who, like the biologist or entrepreneur, does not let emotion sway the work of his intellect in the task at hand, solving a problem of murder as opposed to species mutation or capital utilization. But Holmes at least also much enjoys his pursuit of scientific play ("The game's afoot," he says delightfully, when a case begins to unfold). Whereas teacher Gradgrind teaches indiscriminate and useless "facts," Holmes takes facts to be incidental, others vital to problem solving. And whereas Scrooge reduces life running a counting shop to a boring and uninvolved existence, Holmes isn't happy unless he is engaged in solving a puzzle. The early capitalist movement narrowed experience to the detriment of workers to the point of Luddite and subsequent labor revolts, producing at long last a miserly misanthrope like Scrooge and a cowed subordinate like Bob Cratchit. So by some kind of historical alchemy, economic rationality produced irrational results in the abuse of labor and the mania for gain at all costs, but it also unintentionally created the climate of opinion for the rise of science and for the range of free thought that made for a new form of intellectual play with both scientific and pragmatic results. The ethos of rational organization created both the scientist and the detective, able through scientific play to find out all sorts of things that undermined certainty or exposed criminality.

THE IRONY OF PLUTOCRACY

The modern economic order is based on a special kind of work—directed and disciplined effort in what Weber called a *Herrschaft Verbanden*—an imperatively coordinated association. He thought the rationalized zeal that originated in Puritanism was leading to a secular "iron cage" of endless work and production, a "mechanized petrification, embellished with a sort of convulsive self-importance."[8] The Scroogean descendants of this attitude associated folly with fun. Fun was either sinful or not useful: both the social principles of God and utility supported the redemptive value of earnest effort, and condemned the depredations of folly and mirth. Intimations of the iron cage emerged quickly in the Industrial Revolution, with the rapid growth of bureaucratic institutions—corporations, universities, financial and banking firms, and concomitantly, the state. Work was given both divine sanction and utilitarian force as worthy and proper, a noble calling in which work was its own reward (justifying the meager returns for factory or shop work, farm labor, and such ancillary jobs as teaching). The moral economy included no nonsense about the widespread or "just" distribution of wealth.

The acceptance of economic seriosity was widespread, shared by all economic theorists and apologists, from social Darwinists to socialists. (Karl Marx, author of the grim chapter in *Das Kapital* titled "The Work Day," which outlined the horrors of early capitalism, had a son-in-law named Paul Lafarge who penned a book called *The Right to Be Lazy*, condemning the masochistic lust for work as insane. On publication, the old man was incensed by the proposition that people had an inherent right to goof off, but Lafarge persisted, publishing a journal called *The Idler*, dedicated to the art and science of loafing.) Indeed, the new economic order gave impetus to a new social role, working, and eventually a new social force, the workforce. Laborers became self-conscious of their existence as a class with interests, and labor unions fought to be taken seriously and to be rewarded for their efforts. The rise of both labor and management, for all their struggles and strife, collaborated in creating the contemporary modern economy. The "great transformation" brought about the necessary, if not the sufficient, conditions for the emergence of the play world. Two processes are crucial here: first, the rise and recognition of a wealthy and playful plutocracy, and secondly, the creation of a mass consumer economy.

The accumulation of unprecedented amounts of wealth concentrated in the elite few who owned or otherwise profited from the rise of industry created for them what is sometimes called on "embarrassment of riches." The infamous "robber barons" in America and their slightly more genteel equivalents in Europe were often quite suddenly in the position of possessing enormous amounts of money. And equally as quickly, these newly wealthy headed corporate organizations that did not require their full attention and constant effort. For them, the economic struggle was over, and even though they may not have realized it, they were now so rich they were irrelevant. Corporations such as Standard Oil or I. G. Farben might still be headed by a family, but eventually they came to be owned by stockholders and run by Weber's bureaucrats, functionaries who were skilled at making these imperatively coordinated associations work and produce more wealth.

So what does an irrelevant class of rich people at the top of this economic pyramid do? For this new class of superrich, there was now the question of so much *time* on their hands. If people do not have to work, the options are few. Some sustained the illusion they still were in charge by continuing to "stay on top" of the business; others started new businesses or ventures; others branched out into new careers such as journalism or law or education. But all were aware there was no real *necessity* for work anymore; indeed, they had the enticing opportunity to enjoy free time and creature comforts and exclusive pleasures hitherto known only to the courts and courtiers of antiquity and aristocracies of old. Now it was possible to fill time with *leisure*.

Leisure can take many forms, but the distinction emerged in the early modern social conflicts between vacative leisure, which is enjoyed for its own sake, and recreative leisure, which is instructive and wholesome. The Cavaliers under Charles I published a *Book of Sports,* which permitted certain Sunday sports, infuriating the Puritans; when the Puritans ruled, they banned many leisure activities (a wag noted that the Puritans banned bearbaiting not because they felt sorry for the bear but because they disliked the pleasure it gave to the customers), but permitted those they considered "pure," such as Biblical quizzes. But the dance hall, the public house, and the theater were impure, and Christmas and the Maypole were pagan, so fun and festival were forbidden.

This distinction troubled the new capitalist leisure class, and they tried to contain their enjoyments within the rules of ritual formats such as dinner parties and weekend retreats and genteel etiquette that restricted their pleasures to ladylike and gentlemanly conduct. But their problem was that they had all this time on their hands, and the means for the most erudite and egregious forms of enjoyment. Polite and distinguished erudition could be expressed through art, concerts, travel, and cultivation of the learned and gifted and sophisticated, but they also flirted with more egregious pleasantries, such as endless parties, exquisite dining, mistresses and proteges, coquetry and affairs, and all the temptations of expensive decadence. In other words, the new leisure class had the wherewithal to spend most of its time having fun, both acceptable and outlandish. And many of them did, most famously and extravagantly.

With the modern world committed to the myth of work, and the social fact that most people still had to toil and struggle to make do, the leisure activities of the wealthy became a social sore point of resentment and envy. Socialist rhetoricians sounded like the Puritans of old, damning the irresponsible and lavish funning of the rich and mighty, and conjuring up fantasies of Romanesque orgies and the corruption of pious serving maids. Mass fears and envies were fed by the inaccessible but newsworthy plutocracy, whose kleptomanic accumulation of vast wealth and exhibition of fabulous possessions (mansions and properties, art treasures, ornaments such as horses and servants) became fare for penny presses and muckrakers. The public embarrassment of riches led many of them into good works such as charities, foundations, and displays of a common touch, but their social position and great fortunes remained relatively intact throughout, eventually achieving a modicum of respectability as "old money."[9] The effort was to direct attention away from the vacative leisure deemed as decadent and time wasting, and toward recreative leisure that served social purposes, such as supervising art collections or serving on charitable and university boards (or even go into public life, as the offspring of the Kennedys, Rockefellers, Bushes, and others have done).

But we may wonder whether the attempt to make the rich self-conscious about their fortune was inspired by a recrudescent Puritan asceticism. Rather, it may have been another, more insidious popular interest: what do *we* have to do to live like *them*? The true irony of plutocrats could be their status as a role model, in a dreamlike world of pleasure domes and secular paradises resplendent in their Biltmores and Hyannisports and Kennebunkports and San Simeons. For the emergent middle and professional classes of the last century, the accumulation of modest wealth and a measure of free time brought a question: How do we spend our discretionary money and time? One of the social "places" they could look for cues was this new class of plutocratic rich. Their social practices in the expenditure of vast wealth and great amounts of leisure time could be studied and emulated by their social lessers in less grandiose and extensive ways. In other words, what the many "lessers" wished to know from the "idle rich" was *how to play*, and specifically what kinds of activities constituted fashionable leisure.

The great observer of this process of elite self-dramatization and mass vicarious learning was the social economist Thorstein Veblen, in his *The Theory of the Leisure Class* (1899). Veblen saw that the efficiency-oriented economy of Weber's rational Puritans and energetic capitalists has an ironic outcome. Those who benefit most from the efficient production of goods accrue wealth to the point that they now dignify themselves with honorific status, and deem the indignities of laboring and workmanship that created their wealth as now "beneath" them. Labor is "irksome" because it does not distinguish those who need not work from those who do; thus the roles, and the visible social dramas, of the leisure class are to portray themselves as "above" common labor and devoted to the higher arts of play. To the extent that the leisurely can engage in the "non-productive consumption of time" and dramatic gestures of display, they can be regarded as members of a high-status gentility whose main activity is decorous and exclusive play. For both their class and their admirers among the many, their uselessness is their social use.[10]

Veblen invented some memorable terms to denote their winsome ways: pecuniary emulation, pecuniary decency, conspicuous leisure, conspicuous consumption, and devout observances. These described the very wealthy in late nineteenth-century America, and have been used to describe the rich ever since.[11] Here we wish to stress that these activities, in some ways learned from news and word-of-mouth tales of the superrich, became the activities of the rising middle classes in both large cities and small towns. The pretensions of small towns—exclusive groups such as country clubs and "society"—included the whole inventory of Veblen's analysis: pecuniary emulation in "keeping up with the Joneses," pecuniary decency in adequately expensive gift giving and receiving, conspicuous consumption in buying cars and fashionable clothes, and so on. The point is that at much more bush league levels, the ability to spend much time not working, and much money on luxuries rather than necessities, became a social ideal. The country club, for instance, was an organization in which the sense of distinctive exclusivity could be exercised, and elite leisures such as golf and polo engaged in, just like the superrich who set the standard. By the 1920s, virtually every American town had an elite with aspirations to emulate the leisure class. Activities such as the cocktail party, the dinner-jacket party, the Sunday brunch at the club, sports and games such as golf, tennis, bridge, and backgammon, all filtered down from the symbolic leadership of the leisure class. For the larger society, the superrich leisure class became a social metaphor, conveying the clear message that it is morally permissible to enjoy the benefits of wealth through play. As Veblen indicates, such play dramatizes elite status through pecuniary investment (country club fees, golf apparati, and so on) and conspicuous display (evening gowns, antiques, vacation homes). But elite embrace of the moral permissibility of fun legitimates it for the rest of society. If they can have fun, why can't *we*?

We are a long way from Weber's Puritans, creating capital out of their ascetic duty to save and somberly working long and hard all their lives in earnest pursuit of God's favor and to avoid the temptations of folly, indolence, and pleasure, all the devilments of play. But the appearance of leisure classes as a social ideal suggests the subtle evolution of the modern economy from one function to another. The early modern "Puritan ethic" became the source of the capitalist performance principle, creating rational actors in a market economy maximizing efficiency. But at some point the pleasure principle began to assert itself: we've created wealth enough not to work all the time; when do we get to *enjoy* it? The myth of functional *homo faber* yields to the myth of nonfunctional *homo ludens*. At such points, we may also expect that the role of the economy in society has changed, from the efficient production of goods and services to the creation of wealth as the means to "the good life." We are on the cusp of *consumer sovereignty*.

FABLES OF BEES, ABUNDANCE, AND FUN

The mythic pretext of capitalist authority was that it would create a moral economy. But this assumed it was a more efficient and productive economy of *needs*, providing for those basic necessities of modern life, everything from clothing to farm implements. Originally, then, this pretext was rooted in the ancient doctrine of "production for use." But as Karl Polanyi recognized, the new system was a *market* economy, expanding on "production for gain." This meant "no less than the running of society as an adjunct to the market. Instead of economy being embedded in social relations, social relations are embedded in the economic system."[12] The premise of production for gain suggests that everything can be marketed, since society exists to serve the market. Thus the new system was an economy of *wants*. People can be induced to want more than they need, to acquire things they don't need but are told they should want. The new moral economy was based in the premise that, at least in principle, everything is for sale, and wants can be marketed. Economic morality became a matter of *interest*, based in utility rather than virtue. The new moral system was devoted to creating prosperity and expanding the universe of wants.

Astute observers began to notice this change. In the early eighteenth century, a British physician named Bernard de Mandeville wrote a book eventually titled *The Fable of the Bees, or, Private Vices, Publick Benefits*. He uses the parable of a beehive, in which the prosperity of the hive is dependent upon the individual vices of the bees—greed, sensuality, and pugnacity. The principle applies to hu-

man society: Puritan theologians may preach frugality and austerity and restraint, but social prosperity depends on the exercise of
vice. "It is certain that the fewer Desires a Man has and the less he
covets, the more easy he is to himself . . . [But] what Benefit can these
things be of, or what earthly good can they do, to promote the
Wealth, the Glory and Worldly Greatness of Nations?" (Adam
Smith's *The Wealth of Nations* was influenced by Mandeville.) Mandeville's paradox is that even though we pay lip service to virtue, the
prosperity of material civilization is created by the gratification of
vice! If people did not exercise vices (such as acquisitiveness, vanity,
lust, and quarrelsomeness), the social virtues of prosperity, luxury,
and national power would wither. He presages the consumer economy: "It is the sensual courtier that sets no limit to his luxury; the
fickle strumpet that invents new fashions every week; the haughty
duchess that in equipage, entertainment, and all her behavior,
would imitate a princess." True, he says, "every want was an evil,"
but also, society depends on the "multiplicity of those wants" to further "mutual services." One can imagine what the descendants of the
Puritans thought of his glib remark, "Religion is one thing and trade
is another." Since vice is necessary for the new market economy,
cleverness in appealing to vice is worthwhile. Thus hooped and
quilted petticoats, which appeal to vanity in women and lust in men,
are a luxury that provides for a vast array of related work to produce,
even though they are absolutely nonfunctional, useful only for the
play of coquetry and courtship.[13]

Mandeville still makes people uncomfortable with the argument
that modern society depends on hypocrisy in the gap between what
we profess and what we do, and that prosperity depends on the market's ability to manipulate our baser motives. In the eighteenth century, we begin to see the seeds of the consumer economy, in the
modern attitude toward *choice*. The rise of the market economy paralleled the expansion of political democracy. People began to think
they had a right to choose between candidates as well as products.
Consumer sovereignty and political sovereignty were part of the
same process, resulting by our time in the democratization of economic and political goals. Like political democracy, free trade would
never be complete, but by the nineteenth century, both economic lib-
erals and Marxists thought that the world moved from scarcity to
abundance, from ignorance to knowledge, and from servitude to freedom. The self-regulating market of the social Darwinists and the
communal market of the Socialists would lead to a world of choices,
wherein people could delight in the choice of products, vote for a can-

didate who was eager to cater to their wants, and play a multiplicity of roles. It was no less than Karl Marx who predicted that in the communist utopia, one would be free to choose, since humankind would be liberated from the "division of labor" and live in a "realm of freedom" ("making it possible for me to do one thing today and another thing tomorrow, to hunt in the morning, fish in the afternoon, raise sheep in the evening, and practice criticism after dinner according to my whim . . ."). But Darwinist Herbert Spencer also envisioned a day in which "sympathetic pleasure will be spontaneously pursued to the fullest extent advantageous to all."[14]

These various theories of progress all seem to point to one hope: that the advance of our abilities to conquer nature and change society will lead to a life freed in an unprecedented measure from old necessities in favor of new possibilities. This new possibility would be the enjoyment of play. The ideologies to which we are heir all posited a mythical future of shimmering delights and sympathetic pleasures. The old economies of needs utilized production for use; the new economies of wants posited production for gain to create abundance. Later we shall discuss whether that is now being superceded by *production for fun*.

THE CULTURE OF CORNUCOPIA

The hope of play, then, enters economic thought and becomes a popular ideal. The modern forms of economic organization all attempted to organize effort, utilize technique, and manipulate compliance to maximize gain. Where it was most successful, as in the United States and Western Europe, it brought with it the "problem" of abundance. Societies characterized by widespread abundance not confined to elites were something new. This meant that modern *cultures* had to adapt to the new dynamic of market economies, the existence of leisure classes and ideals, and the great cornucopia of *things*, objects we may not need but do want. Scarcity had been in most times and places the natural order of things. Abundance was the province of the palace or a myth of heaven, amid folktales of the harems and feasts of pashas and potentates, and images of heaven in which all the faithful may share. (Imagings of heaven amongst peoples used to scarcity and poverty are sumptuous: both the Christian and Islamic faiths envision a paradise of plenty, and the play *The Green Pastures* shows an African-American folk heaven of cigars, boiled custard, and a fish fry.) The tribal rituals of sharing and waste called "potlatch" gave symbolic meaning to a period of feast and giv-

ing absent most of the time. Abundance was so rare that it was celebrated in ceremonial form.

Modern economies, then, brought something new into the world: a
mass culture of abundance. The techniques of production and distribution, the spread of mass prosperity, and the competitive market in
available goods and services became a fact of life in many countries
by the mid-twentieth century. As these social facts became clear, the
problem of sustaining such a system required marketing, or the manipulation of compliance. The "engineering of consent" meant the
use of the arts and sciences of *propaganda*, most visibly in advertising and public relations. The experience of the World Wars created
an available executive class skilled in the use of propaganda. But the
job of advertising was to keep the consumer economy going through
the inducements to consume. People were to be told that they needed
what they wanted. The disposition of abundance required that people buy it.

Now this economic reality ran against the grain of some long-
established values and habits. The Puritan heritage emphasized
savings, frugality, and avoidance of luxury and excessive possessions. People had long been taught that since scarcity and hardship
are normal, prudent use of money and property was wise; the impru-
dent squandered their wealth, went into debt, and made unwise purchases of things they didn't need. The advertiser had to create
alternative images of a cornucopia from which good things flow, and
had to convey that wealth is to spend, and that the infinite variety of
goods available made our lives easier, safer, richer, or more pleasant.
From advertising firms flowed a "carnival of exotic imagery" that
represented mundane objects as symbolic things "animated with
meaning."[15] The implicit message from advertisers was "Join the
fun."

Advertising was not far removed from the carnival barker who
lured customers into the sideshow on the promise of wonderful
sights and the hint that if they passed this up, they were dopes for
missing the fun. But advertising's use of the mass media gave widespread and democratic force to the pitch: *everyone can, and should,
join in the fun*. Fear not—consumption is fun. The culture of consumption was defined by advertising as one in which it is permissible, indeed expected, for you to have fun. The old moral economy of
delayed gratification and "saving for a rainy day" vanished under the
lures of advertising. With the onus against debt undermined, the in-
stallment plan, easy mortgage, and loans became common. With the
urgency of enjoyment *now*, there became no insurmountable reason

to wait. People consumed all the pitches of the "Veblen effect": presents had to measure up to pecuniary decency, luxuries such as perfumes or watches were sold as conspicuous consumption, vacations in the fashionable places were conspicuous leisure, and so on. Any obstacle to style, comfort, or pleasure could be overcome by the right product or service: you don't have to wait, you don't have to suffer, you can have fun, you can enjoy yourself, you can dream of riches and pleasure domes and the garden of earthly delights.

These newly legitimated and accessible pleasures also included mass entertainment. Advertisers learned how to induce people to buy not only products, but tickets. The motion picture industry went from nickel arcades to a gigantic industry virtually overnight on the advertised lure of having fun. Despite the recurrent efforts of moralists and reformers to censor or ban movies, the ingenious makers of popular films managed to advertise the promise of excitements so well that popular desires for fun overcame the objections of moral guardians. Formerly, people worked or had "family time" at night; now they went to the movies. When there, they would see "previews of coming attractions," essentially advertisements for new movies coming to that theatre soon. Not only were they there this night to play, but there were tantalizing images of more play to come.

People were also seeing something else: movies were conveying to them images of the good life, the high life, the playful life. Movies were about many things, but one was the fun some people have. A movie might well end with moral redemption and punishment of the wicked—gangsters, sophisticates, harlots, gamblers—but not before they had a lot of fun. A glance back at the movies of the 1920s and 1930s reminds us of the extent to which the movies portrayed, and made alluring, drinking, smoking, and partying—tuxedoes and evening gowns, martinis and manhattans, gambling and flirting, affairs and divorces, penthouses and country mansions. One may have been a poor Okie girl in a gingham dress watching a movie in Muskogee, but she was seeing the stuff that dreams are made of, and learning what constituted good times. For many people, pecuniary emulation and conspicuous leisure were learned at the movies.

Movie fans learned the principles of social play not only from the movies, but also from the stars. Hollywood found very quickly that audiences were much interested in the people who played in the movies. Those promoted and advertised as "stars" existed in a firmament of play, living in mansions, throwing parties, appearing gay and elegant, marrying and divorcing and having affairs, getting into trouble over drink and girls and dips in fountains. Despite recurrent efforts to domesticate the image of Hollywood stars, the fans loved it. The stars were supposed to be fun-loving, since they were mass objects of play. A social scientist once examined the biographical profiles featured in popular magazines from 1901 to 1941. In the earlier periods, the profiles tended to be of "serious men" from politics, business, law, and education, all representatives of the successful world of work. But later on, this changed: the profiles turned to movie stars, sports heroes, newspaper and radio figures, people from the whole "sphere of leisure time." The change was from serious "heroes of production" to "heroes of consumption," figures from the play world of entertainment and leisure.[16] The former represented the earnest attitude and the world of work and success in producing heavy things—money, steel, legalities, degrees—whereas the latter represented the ludenic attitude and the world of play. As the century progressed, the heaviness of the serious world may have seemed more and more forbidding, and the lightness of the play world more appealing. One could identify with the movie stars who lived the lighthearted life of gaiety and elegance. We were compelled to acknowledge the importance of the realm of seriosity in the world of power and wealth and organized effort that gave us a livelihood, but we could voluntarily enter the realm of frolic and sport that gave us a lively time, if only vicariously. We learned to distinguish between "dead earnest" and "living it up," and at least in our fantasies, preferred the latter. Heroes of production continued to fire our ambitions and dreams of pecuniary success, but heroes of consumption fired our fancies about what we could do with money and freedom. The celebrities of Hollywood and "cafe society" taught us that play was not inaccessible, even for those of us with modest means. Social mentoring was moving from the seriously rich and powerful to the playfully famous and sporting. Celebrity stars were in their public beings advertisements for the social principle of joining in the fun.

The culture of cornucopia increasingly offered multiple ways for people to spend their discretionary wealth and time. By midcentury, people in many Western countries were beginning to have disposable income, available time, and a learned inclination to play. We longed to become heroes of consumption ourselves. With the institutionalization of the consumer economy, the necessity of spending became all the more crucial to the maintenance of prosperity. Savings rates often fell to zero, and many middle-class families were in debt most of their lives. More people were mobile up the income and status ladder, and also mobile as to where they lived, with the growth of suburbia and the necessity of relocation. But they were also mobile for playtime, with the automobile giving people unprecedented access to the joys of the open road (and the traffic jam) at parks, vacation sites, drive-ins, indeed the miasma of the "road culture" characteristic of wealthy countries with widespread automobile ownership. (Cars also contributed to the sexual revolution as a vehicle for "parking"; wags have traced the postwar "baby boom" to the back seat of Fords and Chevrolets.)

The culture of prosperity and mobility was also a culture of *immediacy*, in which what was important was what was happening now, the immediate experience. The mass media of communication focused on the immediate, what was going on in the news today, what was fashionable to wear and read and so forth right now, what was fun to do, and what fashionable people were doing it. The "daily fill" of news tended toward sensational headlines, human interest stories, and snappy editorials, complemented by sports and comics and astrology columns. Advertising focused on the immediately fashionable, since propagating the ever-renewable idea of living "up to date," knowing "where the action is," and doing "what's in" at the moment was accorded paramount social importance. In a sense, advertising created the consumer culture habit of shopping. Since "to buy is to be perceived," shopping became a habit of play, wherein one looked for those things that would serve as displays of one's contemporary identity.[17]

In many countries before the Industrial Revolution, the distinction between work and play was unclear, and although days might be long in the shop or field, they were interspersed with time off—many holidays, siestas, and time for games or goofing off. But the organization of the workday into long hours (in the 1830s, by some estimates the workday was more than twelve hours) did demarcate the work week from the weeknight and the weekend, what we now call "free time." Trade unions had a slogan: "Eight Hours for Work, Eight Hours for Rest, and Eight Hours for What We Will." It was the time of "what we will" that was the target of the new consumer economy. The movies were only one leisure-time pursuit; fun parks such as Coney Island and its many imitators became prosperous. The time of "what we will" became for many a daily experience of carnival. Whereas carnival had in previous centuries been confined to a specific period or occasion (e.g., Mardi Gras, or the coronation of a monarch), now carnival time could be enjoyed every evening. Shopping areas such as markets and department stores began to open at nights and on weekends, and the "continuous fair" of open stores and ever-changing goods appealed as a place to go during the time of will.

Shopping and spending became a cultural form of bourgeois theater.[18] The department stores that became important in first urban and then small-town life were famous as stages for displaying the cornucopia of attractive and affordable goods, resplendent with floorwalkers and lobbies and elevators and tubes. Huge stores such as Macy's and Gimbel's in New York, Marshall Field's in Chicago, Nieman-Marcus in Dallas, and Harrod's in London became meccas for aspiring middle-class shoppers eager to see the sociodrama of cornucopia.[19] Chains such as Sears and Montgomery Ward in the United States, and Marks and Spencer and Sainsbury's in England, brought this carnival of collectibles to towns. Such stores were advertisements in themselves, in that just walking through them and gaping at the jewelry and smelling the perfume and feeling the lace of undergarments put one in the mood. The metamessage was, "It's fun to buy neat stuff." In the 1920s, the first malls appeared. The sites for the grand theater of shopping were being built, and the habit of admiring and purchasing things that shore up identity was established. We became what we bought.

So, too, were the sites for the grand theaters of entertainment, equally important for the representation of play. The great movie palaces that began in the 1920s became, like the department stores, elegant settings for play, with exotic or grandiose architecture, uniformed ushers, and an evening of visual entertainment, organ music, and refreshments. The movies themselves propagated the impetus to "screen out the past," whereby they "could infuse life with a new instinctual dynamism and provide a major stimulus for generating modern manners, styles, and models of psychological fulfillment."[20] Similarly, the construction of huge sports coliseums catered to the desire to fill the time of will through sports. Yankee Stadium, the Rose Bowl, Boston Garden, Soldier Field, Madison Square Garden, and so on were all monuments to play, based in the mass desire to see the best athletes at play. Night and Sunday baseball, and soon other sports, developed to correspond with times of will.

With the cultural demarcation of the day and week into times of effort and times of rest and will, Western countries began to conceive of play and leisure as the antidote or "cure" for earnest effort and work (the distinction is less clear in Japan and Latin countries). Recreation became both a value and an industry. National and state parks, recreation areas, city parks and leagues, high school sports, music clubs, and industrial leagues all developed during the first half of the twentieth century as cultural institutions of recreation. With the legitimization of a time of will, it was argued that the masses of people regimented in the daily and weekly routines of effort and labor discipline needed wholesome play to "re-create" themselves and return happily to work. Play here served an extrinsic social purpose: play was deemed good for us, the tonic of fresh air and softball and Sundays walking in the park.[21] Such activities were another choice of play now available, and department stores began to stock elaborate equipment for hunting and fishing and bicycling and musical groups. The social dynamic of play was developing quickly, and produced the inevitable political reaction and conflict.

PLAYING POLITICS

As the modern state developed over the last five centuries, it acquired three distinct if related functions. These were the directive or punitive, the exploitative, and the therapeutic. Modern states were the agencies that directed society, distributed rewards and deprivations, honored and punished, policed at home, and warred abroad. But they also became increasingly involved in directing the exploitation of populations, economies, environments, colonies, and subjects. The state became an agent of prosperity, organizing sustenance, trade, coinage, and taxation. It evolved into the directive institution that not only regulated commerce, but also encouraged it; prosperity was the key to power, so to the extent that the state could stimulate economic growth, the "common wealth" was increased. Progressively, states began to "manage" their economies, with an eye to the political benefits such prosperity could accrue. As modern economies became cultures of gain, the state played a positive role in both social control (maintaining law and order, controlling labor, protecting property) and social prosperity. Countries such as England developed courts of law and domestic police forces, cultivated militaries that controlled the seas and conquered colonies, established mercantilist chartered companies (e.g., the East India Company, the Hudson Bay Company), subsidized science and invention, and sponsored market forces to bring innovations, such as railroads and factories. By the end of the nineteenth century, most modern states were the directive social agent of the common order and the common prosperity. As states became more influenced by democratic forces, these functions had to take into account what was variously called the public interest, the common good, the greatest good for the greatest number—in all cases the democratic principle of giving people what they want, which would increasingly include play.

The development of a unified state under administrative and police control, and a directed economy that sponsored sweeping innovations and labor discipline, occurred at the price of the destruction
of much of the traditional and local organic society. People subjected
to the whims of the market and the anonymity of the city were left in
an "atomistic" state without many traditional supports. And, as
democratic forces developed, people demanded more social and psychic supports from governments. The idea became legitimate that
governments had a responsibility for the well-being of their citizens.
Slowly and often reluctantly, the modern state took on a third function, which for lack of a better term we call the *therapeutic*. Political
therapy involves the government in making a better life for people
under its domain, not only its "welfare state" benefits but more subtly as an agent of social happiness and good feelings. By the late
twentieth century, the state had become not only an agent of prosperity and peace and order, but an agent of morale.

Modern democracies prided themselves on becoming benevolent
states. The function of social control was to be blended with social
justice. Too, the function of social exploitation was united with social
prosperity. And, the function of social morale was linked to social
therapy, the idea that the state should take the lead in the humanis-
tic betterment of people's welfare, both social and psychic. States
were committed not only to an economy of violence and an economy
of effort but also an economy of pain. Peace and prosperity were to be
complemented with the pursuit of happiness. Jefferson's felicitous
phrase may well have been the most consequential political term of
the last two centuries, since it eventually involved democratic governments in the new therapeutic function, attempting to further the
pursuit of happiness and make their citizenry into better persons.
Those many who were abandoned by the industrial and urban revo-
lutions of modernity were "found" by the state and helped, or at least
remolded, by state services. These services ranged from tangible
help with adjusting to the rigors of change, to symbolic help in adjusting to traumatic processes and events.[22]

For political systems, play is obviously something that can serve
the interests of the state. When Wellington remarked that the battle
of Waterloo was won on the playing fields of Eton, he recognized the
political utility of play. The boys playing on those fields were, unbe-
knownst to them, *training*, developing skills useful for military leadership. (Much later, but in the same spirit, Ronald Reagan remarked
on the useful military skills learned in video games.) Sports events
have long been the occasion for patriotic ritual, since the competitive

nature of games seems to symbolize the martial virtues on which military success depends. In this and many other ways, it is never "harmless play," since authorities always attribute meaning, and often danger, to play. Political systems tend to support play that offers affirmative therapy, such as patriotic morale and martial skills. And, since Roman times, states have often utilized the policy of "bread and circuses," providing the masses with food and spectacle. From gladiatorial spectacles to show trials to military parades, state-sponsored play offers diverting and satisfying circuses of fun. Executions—*auto-da fé*, drawings and quarterings, hangings, and so on—were open to the public, which enjoyed the spectacle of official death, but also was reminded of what the state does with miscreants. Play in this sense serves as a form of control, giving political authorities a therapeutic resource with which to manipulate popular opinion.

On the other hand, unauthorized play has often been viewed as dangerous and even treasonous. It is easy to be amused by the extreme efforts to control behavior, including play, on the part of those for whom life is serious and earnest, and frivolity and merriment illegitimate. Such groups in power (the Puritans, the mullahs in Iran, the Taliban in Afghanistan) strike us as applying a religious code of inflexible rules and excessive punishment. Ideals of perfectionism and precision rectitude always run into human frailty and frivolity, so not only weakness but also mere fun becomes unpardonable and subversive. The wrong kind of fun has led to horrific prohibitions and consequences. The Puritans in power became forever infamous for their bans on stage plays (including those of Shakespeare), May Day ceremonies, cards and dicing, minstrels and fiddlers in taverns, and wedding feasts. The Puritan elders insisted that Christmas should be an ordinary workday unobserved, and banned caroling and mistletoe and had ministers searching houses for geese and mince pies. (At one point, the English Puritans decided to ban the religious but not the secular celebration of Christmas, prompting one wag to remark, "O blessed Reformation! The church doors all shut, and the tavern doors all open!") At least one couple was executed for kissing on a Sunday, and severe punishments were meted out for such offenses as dancing and gambling.

Perhaps such an attitude stems from the fear that the therapy of play will lead to "antisocial" behavior. From the Puritans of old to modern totalitarians, this stance views playfulness with suspicion, amidst fears that gaiety and funning will lead to anarchy. Order, the goal of the extremely earnest political attitude, is threatened by the suspect irreverence of playing, which leads to the abyss of impiety and anarchy. Play is associated with anarchy, seriosity with order; truly useful social therapy stems from earnest effort and serious busy-ness. If play threatens to become rebellion, those idle hands that may become the devil's workshop must be occupied. Movements from muscular Christianity to Maoist Red Guards (and even American welfare reform) think that salvation lies in effort, and that idleness presents a social danger. Conservative welfare reformers regard work as the best therapy for idle individuals.

This fear of the disruptive power of play is perhaps most evident in the recurrent social fantasy of sexual anarchy. Especially in periods of cultural anxiety and change, both women's and men's sexual behavior comes under scrutiny as a potential anarchic threat to social order. In the late nineteenth century, the rise in political and social demands by women gave voice to the fear of aggressive, devouring women whose sexual liberation threatened male dominance and the institution of the family. At the same time, the awareness of male homosexuality (as in the trial of Oscar Wilde) and prostitution of both sexes (as in the Jack the Ripper murders) increased the apocalyptic sense of sexual disorder. Advocates of "free love" such as Victoria Woodhull appeared to political authorities as dangers to serious institutions, as did those males (such as London clubmen) who frequented "sporting houses" or clubs with boys. More generally, periods of moral panic lead to clampdowns on play—criminalizing sexual behavior, closing down dance halls or whorehouses, anything that threatens to contribute to the descent into sexual anarchy.[23]

The difficulty with such moral panics is that those who conduct the crusade to "clean up" society are put in the position of being against fun. In increasingly democratic societies, there is a libertarian impulse at work that is difficult to resist: whatever is popular is all right. Moral authorities conducting rituals of purification are often branded as bluenosed pious Puritans, essentially hypocrites at heart and just envious of all those people having all that fun. That may be unfair, but it appeals to the democratic strain that asserts the freedom of play choice, even if it is bad for us (in the United States, this is often expressed as, Who the hell are you to tell me what I can or cannot do?). And, as play has become increasingly considered therapeutic, resistance to play is put on the defensive. With the popularization of Freud, sexual "repression" was deemed bad, and a whole literature of pop psychology developed, arguing that sexual expression—the joy of sex—was both fun and good for you. The sex industry, such as Playboy Enterprises, burgeoned with this irresistible association of pleasure and health. Even activities that are demonstrably bad for you, such as overeating and smoking, invite resistance, and crusaders attempting to stamp out such unhealthful activities are stigmatized as "new Puritans." Dieticians are branded as Puritans attempting to stamp out the fun of food and drink, and a hearty laugh goes up when news emerges about the healthful benefits of alcohol and rich food.

The twentieth century, then, was witness to political struggles over the status of play in society. In many cases, such conflicts were sites of *symbolic politics*, wherein the status of play was at stake as a symbol for certain social values.[24] The fear that play is dangerous led to controversies and struggles for power over play. Prohibition was not limited to alcohol; many American states and communities banned books, dancing, gambling, and an array of sexual acts, and passed Sunday "blue laws" forbidding certain purchases and activities on the Sabbath. The difficulty was, reprising our discussion here, threefold: there was a market for play, there was time and money for play, and eventually there was a political rationale and demand for play. The market for play meant that influential economic interests could overcome local prohibitions against, for instance, Sunday closing laws, liquor by the drink, and the sale of condoms. The availability of play became a social demand for the many who sought places to play, such as parks, lakes, theaters, stores, and so forth. And with the political legitimization of play, it became difficult to resist the asserted *freedom to play*, the principle that people could do with their free time pretty much what they wanted, and that objections to such freedom were an illegitimate interference in personal choice. Appeals to the liberty of "consenting adults" or "privacy" began to appear as individualistic defenses of play. The principle of "possessive individualism"—that the individual in modern market society is proprietor of his or her own person—persists in our belief in our own self-interest and freedom of choice, including more than ever the freedom to play.[25]

The freedom to play came to be complemented by the asserted *obligation to play*. Since play was both legitimate fun and good for us, we had to play as part of our obligation to live the rich, full life that was the democratic promise. Just as the moral economy was superceded by the consumer economy, "goodness morality" was gradually overcome by *fun morality*. Rather than the delay or prudent exercise of gratifications, now the morality of fun justified the immediacy and imprudence of "letting loose" in the present. Those incapable of such impulses (shopping sprees, rounds of parties, happy hour gatherings, flirtations, and easy sex) were in danger of a new kind of social stigma, of not being "with it." Inhibitions no longer denoted a moral fear of guilt ("I shouldn't do that") that guided behavior; rather they suggested a moral lapse producing anxiety ("What is wrong with me that I can't have fun?"): "Whereas gratification of forbidden impulses traditionally aroused guilt, failure to have fun now lowers one's self-esteem."[26] The shift from guilt to self-esteem suggests social movement from the heaviness to the lightness of being.

Similarly, the goal of concerted social energy shifts from use to gain to play. This is what we meant by *production for play*: utility and accumulation both have their roots in human need and human greed. But the newer ethos organized working around the hope of playing, purchasing around the fun of consuming, and accumulating around the learned habit of spending. As fun morality spread, it became easier to resist the fun police who urged parsimony and restraint. The new economic culture that emerged subtly rearranged the motive for effort, the goal of economy, and the basis of culture. Mandeville's bees were allowed to enjoy the honey of the hive, and this enjoyment was deemed a social good.

The dynamic of play, then, was not only the gradual expanse of widespread discretion over play, but also the social incorporation of *play as a value*. Play became something that we not only wanted to do and preferred to do, but also something that we valued doing. If play was both fun and therapeutic, then the freedom to engage in play became something we could possess. It became a measure of freedom and social power to the extent that one could find the time to play and the wealth to engage in fashionable or elegant play. For the democratic many, freedom to play was an innovative idea that transformed a formerly marginal or exclusive activity into a social symbol. When play was accorded status as a valued possession, then we were well on the way to its social elevation in the present, to which we now must turn. Our next question is, Given that play developed into an important and vital social activity, how is it being conducted now?

NOTES

1. Harold Lasswell, "General Framework: Person, Personality, Group, Culture," in *The Analysis of Political Behavior* (New York: Oxford University Press, 1948), pp. 200–230. See also Heinz Eulau, "H. D. Lasswell's Developmental Analysis," *Western Political Quarterly* 11 (June 1958): pp. 229–242.

2. Max Weber, *The Protestant Ethic and the Spirit of Capitalism* (London: George Allen and Unwin, 1930).

3. Hannah Arendt, *The Human Condition* (Chicago: University of Chicago Press, 1958).

4. Werner Sombart, "Capitalism," *Encyclopedia of the Social Sciences,* vol. 3 (New York: Macmillan, 1933), p. 345.

5. Kirkpatrick Sale, *Rebels Against the Future* (Reading, MA: Addison-Wesley, 1995); E. P. Thompson, *The Making of the English Working Class* (New York: Vintage Books, 1966).

6. Charles Dickens, *Hard Times* (New York: Penguin Classics, 1985); Dickens, "A Christmas Carol," in *Christmas Books of Charles Dickens* (Roslyn, NY: Black's Readers Service, n.d.), pp. 5–100.

7. Robert Merton, "Puritanism, Pietism, and Science," in *Social Theory and Social Structure* (New York: The Free Press, 1957), pp. 574–606.

8. Max Weber, *Protestent Ethic*, p. 182.

9. Nelson W. Aldrich Jr., *Old Money: The Mythology of America's Upper Class* (New York: Vintage Books, 1989).

10. Thorstein Veblen, *The Theory of the Leisure Class* (New York: Funk and Wagnalls, n.d.).

11. Lewis H. Lapham, *Money and Class in America* (New York: Ballantine Books, 1988).

12. Karl Polanyi, *The Great Transformation* (New York: Rinehart & Co., 1944), p. 57.

13. Bernard de Mandeville, *The Fable of the Bees* (London, 1705–1723). See Neil McKendrick, John Brewer, and J. H. Plumb, *The Birth of a Consumer Society* (London: Europa, 1982).

14. Karl Marx, *The German Ideology* (1845–46); and Herbert Spencer, *An Autobiography*, vol. 1 (New York: D. Appleton & Co., 1904), p. 25, is cited in *Karl Marx: Selected Writings*, ed. T. B. Bottomone and M. Rubel (New York: McGraw-Hill, 1956), p. 258.

15. Jackson Lears, *Fables of Abundance* (New York: Basic Books, 1994), pp. 8, 10. See also James E. Combs and Dan Nimmo, *The New Propaganda* (New York: Longman, 1993).

16. Leo Lowenthal, "Biographies in Popular Magazines," in *American Social Patterns,* ed. William Petersen (Garden City, NY: Doubleday Anchor, 1956), pp. 63–118.

17. David M. Potter, *People of Plenty* (Chicago: University of Chicago Press, 1954); William E. Leuchtenburg, *The Perils of Prosperity, 1914–1932* (Chicago: University of Chicago Press, 1958).

18. Jean-Paul Sartre, "Beyond Bourgeois Theatre," in *Theatre in the Twentieth Century,* ed. Robert W. Corrigan (New York: Grove Press, 1963), pp. 131–140.

19. Hugh D. Duncan, *Communication and Social Order* (New York: The Bedminster Press, 1962), pp. 347–369.

20. Lary May, *Screening Out the Past* (Chicago: University of Chicago Press, 1983), p. 238.

21. Witold Rybczynski, *Waiting for the Weekend* (New York: Viking Penguin, 1991).

22. Philip Rieff, *The Triumph of the Therapeutic* (New York: Harper Torchbooks, 1968).

23. Elaine Showalter, *Sexual Anarchy: Gender and Culture at the Fin de Siecle* (New York: Viking Penguin, 1990).

24. Murray Edelman, *The Symbolic Uses of Politics* (Urbana: University of Illinois Press, 1967); Orrin E. Klapp, *Collective Search for Identity* (New York: Holt, Rinehart, & Winston, 1969).

25. C.B. Macpherson, *The Political Theory of Possessive Individualism* (London: Oxford University Press, 1962).

26. Martha Wolfenstein, "The Emergence of Fun Morality," *Journal of Social Issues* 7, no. 4 (1951): p. 14. See also Daniel Bell, *The Cultural Contradictions of Capitalism* (New York: Basic Books, 1978).

CHAPTER 2

The Pragmatics of Play

In the previous chapter, we treated the development of play at a rather breathless pace and used a somewhat highfalutin' conceptual inventory. But if the reader has grasped something of the dynamics of play—how play developed out of the history of modernity and became a central social fact—then she or he is well on the way to understanding something important about our current time and condition. Now we must turn to that present—the late twentieth and early twenty-first centuries—to understand the contemporary uses of play in our world of "advanced" or "late" modernity. In other words, what do we *do* with play in the present? If play has become as important as we have argued, then what value do we place on it, and how do we practice it? This is why we term the continuation of our inquiry into play the *pragmatics* of play. For in any present, play as a social fact invites action. People are for it or against it, agree or disagree about it, value it or devalue it, engage in play or eschew it, and reflect on play (as we are doing here) or choose to ignore it. Before we proceed, let us reiterate: we are living in a time and place in which play has taken on unprecedented importance, so much so that as a social principle and practice it has become increasingly central to the conduct of our lives. How do we play now?

TRIPPING THE LIGHT FANTASTIC

Let us continue with our concept of "heavy" and "light." If we look back at earlier modern periods, we associate them with heaviness—economic development, cultural hegemony, and political empires. The development of modern corporations, financial institutions, cultural institutions, and political dominions involved the organization of earnest endeavor directed at creating systematic domains of power. The history of, say, England over the last two centuries is a prime example, with the creation of corporations (British Petroleum), finance (the Bank of England, Lloyds of London), cultural institutions (universities, museums, the Church of England), and the unified state and empire (the Houses of Parliament, the Royal Navy, the vast imperial administration). These systems of power did heavy things, such as processing and selling oil and gasoline, controlling money and providing insurance, administering education, and ruling territories and peoples. This involved the rational application of technique by managerial classes to the coordination of earnest effort. Large populations in modern countries are affected by these large systems—working for corporations, buying products from them, borrowing money, going to public schools, attending Hollywood movies, depending for our health on the medical industry, and paying taxes to the state. In late modernity, many such organizations have become so large and remote from the individual that they invite recurrent populist revolts and expressions of alienation.

The phenomenon of big organizations with great power to influence and direct us has been termed "systematization," integrating large populations into habits of predictable control and compliance. At the same time, habits of "differentiation," human choices and values that make us distinct and different, also have persisted.[1] Our identity as individuals and group and community members involved activities distinct from systems of power gave our lives their differentiated meaning. Many such activities involved "civic engagement" with family and groups—reunions, clubs, churches, unions, and so on. It has been argued that recently, many such traditional activities are in decline. People are allegedly more disengaged from family, and much religious and political rhetoric is expended decrying familial decay and vowing to resurrect "family values." Similarly, people are thought to engage less in civic activities such as voting, community service, and the like. There is even evidence that church attendance is much lower than previously estimated. Now, in many cases older forms of activity have just been superceded by new ones (the ham radio replaced by the Internet, Little League replaced by soccer), but there is abroad a great sense that people are disengaging from those differentiating activities that make life meaningful.[2]

The reason for this is no doubt complex, but a clue to the puzzle lies in two concurrent trends in the way we live in late modernity, in America and in many other places, such as Europe and Japan: the systemic demands of work and responsible action, and the differentiating demands of play. We spend more time working in the systems of effort we have described, and we also spend more time playing in the systems of leisure that have arisen. Our day is increasingly precluded by the time spent at jobs and careers, and by the time spent at the felt necessity to play. Both work and play have become both choices and obligations; we choose to work hard and long to "make a living" and play hard to "have a life," but also feel obliged to work and play as *means of self-expression*. We can't "have it all" or "enrich" ourselves unless we have fulfilled ourselves through both our careers and our leisure times. Especially for ambitious people in the professional classes, the "time crunch" stems from their ardent desire to express themselves adequately in both their vocations and their avocations. Both political rhetoric and commercial advertising assure us that yes, we can have it all, in the sense of high compensation for work and high expectations for play. We are not content with either poverty at work or poverty at play; both are supposed to make us richer, with both material and psychic rewards as sought and deserved enrichments.

It is often said that people determined to fill up time with activity are "driven."[3] Determination drives them to succeed at jobs and careers, putting in long hours and bringing work with them wherever they go. From local entrepreneurs to high-powered Wall Street financiers and Washington attorneys, career self-expression involves a crushing commitment to long hours. Play becomes mixed with work: executives playing golf discuss deals, people using their car phones and fax machines on trips, couples working on their computers during dinner, office workers eating lunch in their cubicles, and so on. The phenomenon of overwork is not confined to Americans; whereas the business district in London called "the City" used to have casual hours and much time off, now it is superbusy and hours are superlong. (Recall that Marx's famous chapter on "The Work Day" in *Kapital* saw the proletariat working endless hours while capitalists had much leisure; now the most highly educated and paid work brutal hours and often have no social life to speak of, and the poor and uneducated work sporadically, if at all.) This has led to the conclusion that leisure is in decline, although some observers think this is confined to the well-off professional classes driven to succeed and accumulate.[4]

So where does this leave play? For the driven, play becomes obligatory, either for professional reasons (joining a club) or as an expression of wealth or fashion (vacationing at the "in" place). But even
when playtime is not so compromised, the principle of determined
drivenness often obtains. It is easy to observe, say, a family outing at
a theme park. Armed with a block of tickets, the family enters the
systematized place—Disney World, Six Flags, wherever—determined to have differentiating fun. Thus the day is spent going to all
the attractions, standing in long lines for rides and shows, persisting
all day with the grim resolve to hustle through all the tickets until
everyone is exhausted. They can then return home with the satisfaction that they had good fun, measured by money spent and energy
expended, and that the happy family outing met their criterion of en-
richment. But the outing was not *leisurely*, in the sense of relaxing
and slowly paced diversion. The driven do not associate play with relaxation. Loafing, napping, or doing nothing is not an option; time
has to be "full" of some sort of activity toward a goal, usually defined
as winning or achieving—winning at handball, climbing a mountain,
making the deal on the eighteenth tee, using up all the tickets, always "playing hard." (When people are asked in polls to name their
favorite leisure activities, "relaxing" comes in dead last.) In our time,
many people are driven to play. For a wide variety of motives, they do
not choose to play; they *must* play, or at least convince themselves
that they are capable of, and prepared for, play.

In the "speed culture" of today, the distinction between earnest effort and playful activity has become blurred. But since both are
means to self-expression, this has also meant, at least again in the
professions, that the most desirable worksites and workmates are
those that organize effort as playful, in the sense of creativity and
self-fulfillment. (In the 1970s, polls began to show that people
wanted personal growth and self-expression more than anything
from their chosen careers.) They want the same from playsites and
playmates. The number of vacations and retreats offering such activities as archaeological digs or executive brainstorming with the
latest business guru has expanded. Lawyers now marry lawyers and
doctors, on the premise of combining a firm or practice with a good
spouse. Given professional life at warp speed, it is no wonder most
two-career couples complain the most about "too little time," which
means too little time to complement career demands with play experiences. Perhaps this explains the acquisition of items little used,
such as state-of-the-art kitchens in which no gourmet meals are
cooked and grand pianos that are never played, "virtual leisure,"

wherein exhausted couples at night watch TV shows about home re-
pair or gardening or fishing, and "passive leisure," when tired people
cocoon with videos and delivered pizza or surf the 'Net rather than go
out. If we had the time, we would learn the piano or plant a garden or
hike the Appalachian Trail, but all many of us have now is the vicarious experience of activities in which we do not participate, lacking
the time and energy for leisurely enjoyment or even for minimal
pleasures such as exercise or cooking a meal. So the exercise machine becomes a coat rack and the cat sleeps undisturbed on the
stove.

There is, however, much evidence of a great deal of dissatisfaction
among hardworking people: bad bosses, cubicle life, management
fads, impenetrable technology, downsizing, the whole dreary litany
of working woes. (The popularity of the comic strip *Dilbert* gives us a
major clue to the state of the workplace.) For the many who are not
part of the professional elite that commands stratospheric compensation, the rewards of work, in terms of both money and fulfillment,
are often less than satisfactory. People can stand a great deal of pain
and idiocy at work if there are big rewards, but relative earnings
have become stagnant, and moonlighting and deep debt are common.
More cosmically, people are also aware of the inequalities and uncer-
tainties of the new economy: we now speak of the zero-sum society,
the winner-take-all economy, in-your-face capitalism, the overclass,
and the like. There are dark forecasts about the workerless corporation, the "end of the labor society," the elimination of labor as the next
great economic agenda.[5] For this reason, people at various levels
work hard and accumulate wealth to achieve not only recognized
success, but also success, they hope, at eventually freeing themselves
from the necessity of work for the pleasures of play. *We work in order
to play, eventually.* The irritant of consuming work life is the question, "When do we get to play?" The dissonance of professional existence is the constant necessity to keep delaying ludenic gratification.
The great dream that drives us on is the hope of eventual time to play
at our leisure and of our choice. We envision early retirement, golden
parachutes, trophy wives, golf communities, the golden years, worka-
holics transformed into playaholics. Money doesn't buy happiness,
we know, but it can buy us the opportunity to play. TV financial advertising (mutual funds, financial management firms, on-line trading) emphasize mature play as a reward for a career of accumulation,
with images of healthy retirees in their maturity having affluent and
active fun. The point of work and accumulation is to free us from the
rigors we endured: "Now it's playtime," say the ads showing mature

but energetic and handsome people in big new cars or exploring foreign climes or funning on cruise ships. "Pleasure got mad at work,"
says the ad from the California tourist authority. "Said, I'm leaving . . . work isn't laughing now. . . . Pleasure says, 'Wish you were
here.' " In the contemporary economy, work expands to eventually
buy the time to play.

It is not necessary to belabor—or is it beleisure?—the fact that often those freed up for play don't have a clue about what to do with
free time or even how to have fun once they have "earned" it. Those
for whom life has been a serious career and drive for advancement
and hours of labor never developed the habits and skills needed for
play. Often they have lost the ability for spontaneity or enjoyment, so
ironically, after expending much sweat to get to the point of funning,
they haven't a clue about how to have fun. In the past, the difficulty of
the transition was a movement from heavy to light activity. Both
steel magnates and steelworkers had trouble dealing with both freedom and play. But now we live in a light economy increasingly dominated by "symbol analysts" who mix work and play, so perhaps they
can deal with such changes in their lives, or simply collapse the cate-
gories of work and play so that no transition is necessary. Nevertheless, the benefactors of the new economy as much as their
predecessors accept the myth of play as reward, the hopeful fantasy
that their lives can be enriched by play and will culminate in play as
the payoff of achievement. As long as the siren song of advertising
lures us into tripping the light fantastic of play, then the driven will
drive themselves to a point where they do not have to drive anymore.
It will require that lead-footed heavies learn how to dance lightly
again.

But in a driven culture, it remains difficult for those committed to
heavy tasks to find time for play as they live their productive lives.
We are in an era of the "fall of fun," in which many people, including
the best and brightest in creative fields, find it hard to lighten up and
enjoy themselves in the ludenic interstices of life. Play remains a
shimmering potentiality, but one never quite gets around to it. And
in the wake of that new version of Puritanism called "healthism,"
moral judgments are legislated or informally imposed with the
authority of public health, wherein pleasures are medicalized, stig-
matizing every mild narcotic, even art, into an issue of public health
and social morality. Once, the great writers and thinkers and journalists were inveterate drinkers and smokers and drug takers and
sexualists, carousers and libertines and bohemians who were intent
on having fun along the way, often to heroic excess. One thinks of the

ebullient hedonism of Ernest Hemingway, the booze and the women and the hunting and fishing, or the gleeful sensuality of Edna St. Vincent Millay, with her candle burning bright at both ends. Part of the adventure of life for those who survived economic depression and world war was interspersing work and achievement with intense fun, often quite sustained and even destructive fun. But they were committed not only to achieving, but also to the pleasure of living fully, including the alternative to unbutton and raise pluperfect hell. But in a social atmosphere of healthism, play is justified only if it contributes to achieving "personal growth" or betterment through strenuous mental or physical effort, and every pleasure, such as martinis or cigarettes or steaks or sex, is stigmatized as an "addiction" from which we must be cured. It wouldn't have occurred to previous generations that something was wrong with such widespread pleasures, but under the repressive regime of healthism, as Russell Baker remarked, the new health police would have made Omaha Beach into a smoke-free zone. (Antihealthism rebels have even formed clubs in which "blows for freedom" are struck by consuming dry martinis and cigars and marbled steaks.)[6]

The medicalized strictures against play stem from a kind of pseudoscientific morality, but with a mythic base in the belief that the wages of sin are death. Gatherings of artists and intellectuals and celebrities used to be blowouts, but now they tend toward tame wine and cheese and "healthful" fare on the buffet table. By most accounts, Hollywood parties now have all the verve of a church social, with the stars talking about their diets and trainers and cholesterol counts; the Errol Flynn and Tallulah Bankhead hell-raisers of old would be embarrassingly out of place. Rather than living in the bohemias of cities, writers are now indentured as university professors ("writers-in-residence") who move easily in philistine educational circles rather than the covert gatherings of the avant-garde. One suspects that all these creative or important people eschew the intensity of play because they take themselves and what they do *seriously*, and thus are unwilling to take the risks involved in intense and daring play since it would affect their reputations and thus privileged position. But it does seem astonishing and ironic that so many people with talent and wealth and good health seem so incapable of enjoyments that previous generations so relished. The "cultural elite," compared with the predecessors in the twentieth century, seem a pretty dull bunch.

Leadership in the tradition of excessive and spectacular consumption, then, has shifted to other venues—rock stars, sports and music

impresarios, a few athletes, criminals, and adventurers. We may
suspect that many intellectuals have been tamed by tenure, writers
by contracts, and celebrities by their publicists. There do remain
some social bastions of bohemian and rebellious life. If the demands
of career and the strictures of therapeutic puritanism become too
much, one can still "drop out." Beach cultures still abound, and people have been known to leave office and home and club behind and
become a beachcomber in the Outer Banks or a surfer in Santa Barbara or a waiter in Mykonos. Similarly, romanticized rebellions such
as joining biker groups or ski or tennis "bumming" offer the embur-
dened bourgeoisie a lure of leaving care and seriosity behind and
"lighting out," like Huck Finn, for some new territory. Former bohemian places, such as Greenwich Village or Haight-Ashbury, famous
for the intellectual rebels and social dropouts who lived there, are
now "gentrified" and unaffordable to the struggling poet or student
rebel. Yet some student cultures still exist wherein one may lead the
life of an "academic bum" who lives the life of an alienated intellectual or at least hanger-on. Those who fantasize about joining such
"alternative lifestyles" see them as play-lives, free and easy ways of
living with plenty of time for fishing or roaming or talking. The
beachcomber or biker or eternal student is envisioned as liberated
from the constraints of how most of us live. But such a vision reminds
us that a major current definition of freedom is the ability to play;
one is free to the extent one can escape the mundane culture and
adopt the lightness of being of subcultures and countercultures. In
this daydream, it is the corporate executive or bankruptcy lawyer
who envies the hard-partying beachcomber or philosophy student.

So we may define one of our contemporary social tensions as a
struggle between the careful and the carefree. The careful are people
dealing with the constraints of social time and the burdens of modern life, acutely aware of the strictures of moral fashion that distinguish between the healthy and the diseased. Their fear of becoming
prematurely careworn makes them envy the carefree, abjuring those
having fun at happy hour and eating prime rib. In the ideology of
healthism, food and drink are either medicine or poison, so the careful can feel morally superior. The carefree also court the possibility of
becoming objects of stigma, condemned by the righteous for irresponsible hedonism and frivolous attitude. Public figures such as
politicians and media stars are subjected to censure by the health
authorities if they display interest in hedonic consumption or flout
the discipline of health. Stigma is attached to those who violate these
imposed norms of personal purification. Movie stars now feel con-

strained to dry out in the Betty Ford Center, radio demagogues to go on a diet, male politicians to keep away from women. At the popular level, social opprobrium and sanction are directed at pregnant women who smoke, men in groups who whistle at girls, third-graders who "sexually harass" another child, people who eat meat or wear fur, professors who say something "offensive" in class, and so on endlessly. In the social principle of inspection, those who are physically and morally clean can be found out and distinguished from those who are unclean. The healthistic regimen combines seriosity of attitude with strenuosity of exertion, resulting in purity of being. The wages of sin can be discovered in cholesterol counts and stress tests, and those designated as unclean must atone through purifying diet and denial, renouncing the evils of alcohol and drugs and casual sex and rich foods. Such play is folly; only play that is morally or physically uplifting is worthwhile. The fleshly delights of the barroom and bedroom and dining room must be eschewed in favor of the edifications of the hiking trail and aerobics class and therapy session. Theodore Roosevelt's "strenuous life" is now fueled by Perrier water and alfalfa sprouts.

The difficulty with such earnest agendas as healthism is that they occur in an era that makes light of them. In the emerging play culture, *all serious agendas and people are subjected to comic ridicule.* For the earnest, a social or political agenda is serious business designed to make the world a better place. But for the playful, seriosities are the stuff of comedy. The problem that healthism—or any earnest ideology or project—faces is that a growing number of people won't take it seriously. *Everything serious becomes a joke.* Those who would make us healthy in mind and body become objects of hilarity, and what they are trying to do is deemed ludicrous. The counterargument to serious agendas is cast in terms of amused scorn. The imperative to "get serious" about health or politics or whatever is met with ridicule of imperatives and contempt for agendas. The play attitude counters the grave with the ludenic: How can anyone take this sort of thing seriously? Isn't health something to be ruined? Why would I want to die healthy? Can we not conclude that health is bad for you? The healthy may live long because of no booze and steaks and sex, but why would they want to? With this to look forward to, is there any life before death? Similar agendas become laughable fare, doomed by the comic definition of the situation: making fun of something removes it from the realm of seriosity and diminishes it through ridicule. A modal attitude of our time is that the earnest among us are funny, and that earnest agendas invite not applause or discussion but satire.

It may well be that the period encompassing the last three decades of the twentieth century and some of the first half of the twenty-first century will be remembered for its satiric literature and sardonic attitude. The most potent and pervasive form of popular culture is light comedy, and many venues—stand-up comics, radio talk hosts, syndicated columnists, satirical newspapers—subject virtually everything and everyone to savage satire. Freed from romantic beliefs and even moral indignation, every sacred cow and social activity is reduced in stature by the play of satiric attack. The universalizability of making fun of things is complete, ranging from presidents to paupers, the healthy and the sick, the elect and the damned. The attitude is evident in TV situation comedies, with a typical group of neighbors and relatives skewering everything through the wisecrack. But this ironic stance suggests none of the moral outrage of traditional satire; rather, it mocks all things earnest, including moral stances. This contemporary attitude is playful in the sense that it recognizes of the grotesque and absurd in society, but it is couched only in terms of hip knowingness that snickers at everything defined as fair game.

The contemporary definition of the play attitude, then, tends toward rhetorical sarcasm and social derision. The consequence has been to *expand significantly the field of the risible*. The risible includes all those things we are allowed to openly laugh at, and once universalized, means that we cannot take anything seriously. Assertions of seriosity invite rhetorical play, subjecting high seriousness to low comedy. Those important personages society used to term "serious men"—politicians, clerics, businessmen, educators, the traditional idols of production—are now all subject to pie-in-the-face humor. Older people who were taught to respect the powers that be are often shocked by the offhand comic contempt shown them by stand-up comics and other popular communicators. This prevalent attitude likely began with our vicarious experience with celebrities, journalists, and athletes, the range of idols of consumption. In the latter part of the twentieth century, we began to know more about them as the veil of respect lifted. Our thirst to know about the private lives of the great was sated by newsy gossip. When we learned that movie stars and baseball players and the like were drunks or lechers or simply ordinary, their aura of authority vanished. They were transformed from objects of admiring respect into objects of amused contempt. Rather than hate them or ignore them, we decided to ridicule them. By extension, the same process has happened to serious men (and women). As the relentless probe of inquiry into their true selves and private conduct revealed, or at least intimated, the worst, they became targets of ridicule. This attitude makes it difficult for serious men to sustain themselves as authority figures, since they have become amusing play-figures. Social power is difficult to exercise in an atmosphere of trivialization, since we think them neither powerful nor even sinister, but rather, merely preposterous. As figures of play, they are all deemed equally silly, mere caricatures of eminence. The effort to be "taken seriously" becomes a virtual invitation for satirical attack and character assassination, to be made the butt of a thousand jokes.

Ridicule, then, has become our expressive defense against seriosity. Buoyed by our sense that the world is an absurd comedy and that those who lead us are grotesque, we find it more fun to be frivolous, and wish to banish seriosity and its agents from consideration. Agendas of Puritan therapeutics such as healthism are resisted because they involve adherence to a regimen that is "good for us" and thus is deemed dreadfully strenuous and therefore no fun. Satirical funning becomes an expression of rebellion against those forces and agents who threaten to make life less fun. Such a pervasive attitude obviously has consequences for the introduction of reform agendas, social discipline, and serious discussion. This play attitude influences and reciprocally reinforces both our personal and media communications. Our criterion for evaluating every proposed change or innovation is no longer so much a question of fear of change ("What will I have to do?") or self-interest ("What's in it for me?") as it is play ("Is it any fun?"). *We now seek those communications that support the proposition that life should be fun.*

LET ME ENTERTAIN YOU

Those communications largely emanate from the great school of society, the popular culture. The institution of school may be the formal agency of earnest education, but it has long been eclipsed in importance and influence by the vast informal agency of learning, all those popular messages communicated playfully. The field of popular culture is much greater than, although inclusive of, the media of communications, including all those activities and institutions that involve play. Popular play is the culture of the populace, and is likely the major source of learning in contemporary late-modern society. Expanding on Neil Postman, we may term popular culture as the "first curriculum," the primary source of learning in society.[7] Popular culture is by definition popular, and it is so because it promotes the experience of play. Its power as a source of learning is that it is *entertaining*, communicating the play of musement for popular delight and instruction. The entertainer amuses and teaches through diversion, whereas school attempts to educate through edification. School may occupy the official and moral high ground, but popular culture has everyone's attention. School may be the transmitter of eternal, or at least officious, verities, but popular culture occupies the low ground of immediate experience. We now learn more from popular culture than from school because it is more fun. The institution of school and the school of popular experience do share in common one significant feature: both are highly ritualized. School is ritualized work, transforming learning into routines of strenuous and solemn duties. Popular culture is ritual play, creating forms and formulas of play for immediate activity and opening a vast playground of learning. Much of that learning is incidental and even random, since popular attitudes are caught, not taught in the "covert culture." But popular learning does have patterns, gleaned across populations from the ritualized forms and contents of cultural fare. Those attitudes that are caught make up a kind of "popular logic," involving premises and conclusions drawn by people from both personal and popular experience.[8] If school conveys the official logic of the overt culture, popular culture communicates, and for many, validates, the popular logic of covert and "unofficial" culture. Offering learning through play, it acquires the status of unsanctioned learning, often impressively conveyed through the dramatic power of popular stories and characters. Popular culture offers rituals of power that give force and logic to attitudes that may have been amorphous or unarticulated. If school offers "top-down" learning and lore, popular culture contrasts with "bottom-up" visions and views.

These alternative sources of learning may help explain many contrasting attitudes and behaviors among people simultaneously exposed to both school and popular culture. As an agency of civilization, school attempts to convey civil attitudes: patriotism, deference to authority, law and order, compromise and conciliation as social mechanisms of peace, civic values such as democracy and liberty, and general behavioral values such as fair play and respect for others. These are earnest attitudes with the force of official sanction and institutional propagation. The culture of the populace is much more uncivil. Everything from movies to video games to sports conveys the message that if you want to win, you have to aggress against someone else. The popular culture has long entertained the idea that violent solutions, usually by force of arms, are the way to get what you want. A century of Western movies and books, police and private-eye tales, the folklore of G. I. warfare, sports such as football and hockey, the covert youth culture of bullying and fisticuffs and gangs, all perpetuate the popular ethic of violence. For some impressionable people, popular culture legitimates violence as playful, as a powerful social tactic that achieves results. The formulaic ritual of power is forever repeatable: the wicked are punished, evil is expunged, and a clear and just solution is imposed. The authorities at school may warn against the resort to violence as antisocial and unlikely to play out the way one saw it on TV—people do shoot back—but popular culture has people's attention. *The entertainment curriculum teaches through play, and conditions our expectations about the world.*

The social curriculum of play makes us responsive to those who entertain us. School is designed to be a serious institution, urging on us the earnest curriculum of official values and organized effort. But youths learn quickly the educative value of popular culture, and as wags have it, come to resent school because it interferes with their education. The "metamessage" from school is "Let us edify you." By contrast, the unspoken message from popular culture is "Let us entertain you." The social principle of play is by now largely translated into entertainment values. We are now in "the age of show business" in which "entertainment is the natural format for the representation of all experience," with the presumption that all discourse "is there for our amusement and pleasure."[9] Since being entertained is now a dominant motive and desire for large populations, a massive industry has arisen and expanded to cater to the *play want*. People want play, and entertainment has become the "natural format" for the satisfaction of all those yearning to have fun. And that format has encroached on the activities of formerly serious institutions. The demand for play is now conjoined by an ever-expanding supply of entertainment.

The time crunch is made all the more difficult for contemporary people by the enormous growth in recent decades of the "entertainment economy."[10] We refer here not only to the older media industries, but to new forms of entertainment, such as theme parks, entertainment towns and districts, casinos, sports coliseums, video and interactive games, and so on. This is the ultimate light economy, since it sells the means to become light hearted and often lightheaded. The "business of fun" offers us a wide variety of choices, all widely advertised, that guarantee a good time. As we move from a heavy to a light economy, the entertainment industry promises to be one of great growth. Instead of steel we make sitcoms. We turn defunct downtown business districts into play places for partying or shopping, variations on the French Quarter or Main Street. As factories close and rust, sports complexes and enclosed malls are built. "Enterprise zones" have been a flop, but entertainment zones are a rousing success. When the Dow Jones Industrial Average began in 1896, it was dominated by railroads and steel and oil companies; by the 1900s, it had removed U.S. Steel and Bethlehem Steel and replaced such heavy firms with Disney. And the new economy of communications and Internet companies—Microsoft and America Online and Dell Computer—threaten to make the old economy and old measures irrelevant.

The Disney Corporation has become one of the metaphorical corporations of the new economy. Beginning with Disneyland, the now worldwide company built and marketed fun places dubbed "the happiest places on earth." The themed attractions gave great impetus to the myriad of theme parks that proliferate in entertainment zones: Myrtle Beach, Pigeon Forge, Branson. EuroDisney in France was less of a financial success, and raised questions about cultural imperialism and American kitsch (one French intellectual called it a "cultural Chernobyl"). Branson, Missouri, has become a mecca for tourists eager for virtually continuous entertainment, with shows morning, afternoon, and night, featuring country and western revues, star theaters, cruises, and museums, interspersed with all-you-can-eat buffets. Many other sites in the United States began to have dreams about imitating the success of Branson, attracting retirees, family vacationers, and popular music fans to yet another entertainment zone. As "baby boomers" retire, those with discretionary income may well spend their time and money traveling to such sites, with parking lots full of recreational vehicles and tour buses.[11]

Such contemporary entertainment zones seem qualitatively different from the fun places of yesteryear—amusement parks such as Coney Island, vaudeville halls, movie palaces, penny arcades, dance halls, circuses and carnivals, Barnum-type museums. But they do share Barnum's idea of creating a "sinless carnival" in that they tend to cater to good, clean fun and "family entertainment." The "sin zones" like the French Quarter and the beach towns that cater to those on spring break are exceptions, but even there the industry makes efforts to accommodate both those who come to raise hell and those who come on tour. Disney has pioneered not only happy places we can visit, but happy places we can live. Its planned communities are paradigms of the gated communities around the land, which control access to keep out undesirables and plan wholesome activities like a revived Chatauqua. And you can have it both ways: technophiles can live in the futuristic Epcot Center, and technophobes can live in Celebration, a reproduction of a premodern American country village, with a town square and gazebo concerts and a furniture store that sells only antiques and reproductions of antiques. (One might say that in the former, people live in the global village, in the latter, in the local village; what they have in common is that they are phony towns.)

Another of the great transformations so characteristic of the present is the setting and conduct of shopping. Shopping originated as a habit of functional acquisition. People shopped for the narrow range of farm and town needs for survival and minimal decency. But as prosperity created an expanding people of plenty, much shopping changed from a functional to a symbolic activity: one shopped for luxuries rather than necessities. The ubiquitous shopping mall offered shopping as entertainment. As malls developed, the managers of this new kind of entertainment zone became increasingly aware that shoppers were looking for the thrill of the hunt for beautiful and luxurious objects of adornment, and not merely a dress or shoes. The "Veblen effect" meant that shoppers were not always looking for a bargain, but for an experience: buying items of conspicuousness, enjoying elegant surroundings, identifying themselves with the world of wealth and luxury and sensuality and fame. "Entertainment retail" stores (Niketown, Planet Reebok, Warner's) regularly have "store adventures" such as live entertainment, celebrity appearances, and other "in-store spectacles." Like other forms of entertainment, shopping at this level of sophistication has become an aesthetic experience, celebrating the beauty of acquisition.[12]

This kind of shopping requires the creation of a supportive and permissive environment to allay any guilt or shame about acquiring luxuries. One enduring strategy to overcome reluctance to "shop till you drop" is the appeal of fashion. Acquiring luxuriant goods and services far beyond our needs means framing them as worthy because they are fashionable, since in the luxury economy, being valued depends on being up to date, in style, and cool. This is variously deemed "hip consumerism," the "coolhunt," and "flexible accumulation."[13] Fashion becomes a way of entertaining ourselves by acquiring those things that make us up to date, and therefore youthful and knowledgeable of contemporary culture. When a particular cultural group becomes innovative in dress and habit, it is not long before its fashionability becomes part of the larger culture. Counterculture clothes and habits from the "youth culture" of the sixties and seventies filtered their way up the economic and age scale, and soon mature people no longer youths were sporting the dress and flaunting the habits of young people. The principles of hip marketing make the presentation of the dressed and coiffured self part of now. There is also plenty of "square" shopping: "virtual shopping" over cable channels such as QVC combines the easy talk of a bourgeois kaffeklatsch and familiarity with celebrity guests with the purchase of goods, but the atmosphere is decidedly unhip. In all cases, the impulse is to transform fashion merchandising and purchasing into entertainment, where one becomes a kind of sartorial karaoke flaunting one's fashionable self, or transforming constantly refashioned rooms or displaying collections of objects (ranging from art to shaving mugs) for the obligatory tour. By so doing, people or their environs dramatize themselves as either play-figures or denizens of domestic play places.

Perhaps the most remarkable innovation in play places in recent years has been the gambling casino. The older moral economy yielded to many forces interested in the expansion of play, by acquiescing in the legalization of drink, Sunday opening, and relaxation of censorship. But gambling was confined largely to Nevada in America, and casinos such as those in Monte Carlo in Europe. For most people, gambling was confined to the poker night, office pool, or shooting dice and playing the numbers racket. In recent years, gambling has become legitimate and has proliferated at a rapid pace. As the industry began to expand, "gambling" became "gaming," a prettier term that made the activity more palatable. The gaming industry spread to established fun places, such as Atlantic City and New Orleans. It followed the precedent of state lotteries, which were established for benevolent state purposes such as education. As state lotteries became more common and became enormous cash cows for state governments, the habit of gambling became established among populations and in areas hitherto untouched. (The Illinois lottery destroyed the illegal numbers racket in Chicago run by the underworld, but wags noted that the state paid off less generously than the "outfit.") As a panacea for decayed cities or backward areas, the introduction of gambling became irresistible to local decision makers and deprived groups. State lotteries were voted in, entertainment zones proliferated, and groups clamored for the gaming industry to come to town and set up shop. Despite the objections of leading moralists (both liberal and conservative) and the doubts of economists, the political alliance committed to legalized gambling prevailed. The lure of revenue and riches for elites and fun and windfalls for masses was too much to overcome. By the end of the century, most states had lotteries in which billions of dollars were gambled, and the gaming industry was within a day's drive of virtually every American. Gambling became morally and politically permissible when it was perceived to be economically lucrative and socially popular.

This has led to the bizarre consequence of gambling appearing in places undreamed of a few years ago. American Indians won the right to run casinos on reservations, and elaborate gaming facilities quickly began to appear everywhere, with all the service staff tribal members. Gaming corporations, such as Harrah's, run many of them as an investment, but many formerly poverty-stricken Indian areas have prospered. Many other pieces of land were "discovered," as local areas tried to define a reservation; Detroit tried to zone unused acres in downtown as a bona fide Indian reserve, thus amenable to building a casino. Cherokee, North Carolina, is dominated by a Harrah's operation (2,300 video game machines, 60,000 feet of casino space, open twenty-four hours a day, seven days a week, a 1,500-seat Pavilion theater with live entertainment, and a "culturally themed" child-care facility). From Las Vegas to Atlantic City, one of the astonishing features of the new gambling is the effort to market the fun experience as family entertainment. The large casino operations all have elaborate child-care operations, and offer rides and diversions for the kids while Daddy and Mommy are in the casino squandering their inheritance. Gambling boats began to appear on rivers and lakes and oceans, often docked off a down-on-its-luck area such as Davenport, Iowa, or Gary, Indiana. Perhaps most remarkably, conservative, Bible-Belt Mississippi has become a major center of gambling. Towns such as Biloxi, Tunica, and Vicksburg cater to vast throngs of gamblers daily, of all creeds and races; whereas not so long ago, blacks and whites viewed each other warily across police lines, now they view each other warily over poker hands.

The sudden innovation of legitimate gambling has invited explanation.[14] It may have been that the "gambling culture" was always there, only covert; now that it's legitimately available, former closet bettors flock to the casinos. There are now a lot of people with discretionary income—a large upper middle class, retirees, yuppies, and so on, all of whom are finding a new thrill in rolling the dice. Many new gamblers are in fact experiencing a new form of fun, and it may be that once the novelty passes, they will move on to the next fun fashion. In any case, a significant portion of the American population now gambles, from little old ladies buying a lottery ticket to high rollers betting the farm on the last hand. But why now?

Perhaps the appeal of the "luck business" as a form of fun does have a meaning beyond its mere availability. As on their outings to theme parks or shopping malls, those who venture forth to such fun places are trying to buy happiness in the guise of a moment or object of fun. Gambling combines all this—shopping, as it were, in a thematic fun place, and more: as long as you're there, you're trying your luck. And if fortune smiles, you've freed yourself from care by acquiring the acknowledged means of social liberation: money. (Try an experiment: ask your friends what they would do if they won the lottery or a jackpot, and suddenly were rich beyond their wildest dreams. Watch their faces and listen to their dreams, which will likely be fantasies of fun.) Widespread legal gambling prospered in the economic context of the late twentieth century. Most gamblers are not rich and don't expect to be rich; they live in what for many of them is a "scavenger economy" of cruelty and uncertainty wherein everything is for sale and everyone is expendable. Since a chance in life is unlikely by effort (polls have shown that the percentage who agree that hard work pays off has fallen from a solid majority to a shrinking minority in the last few decades), then games of chance are one's only hope, albeit unlikely. If we live in a culture of speculation from top to bottom, then taking the gamble with blocks of lottery tickets or piles of chips is how the individual gambler can hope against hope that he is the one and this is his only chance. Such folks are neither professional gamblers (who know better) nor compulsives (who can't stop), but rather people in the market for a miracle. Perhaps the fun is in the fantasy of miraculous instant riches and entry into the leisure class, but it keeps the slot machines whirring.

It may also keep the stock investors plunking down money. The small-time gambler may not be very different from the many millions who play the market for fun and profit but who also dream of hitting it big. The market metaphor obviously extends to stock speculation (and futures, commodities, and so on), but it also extends to gamblers, who are, after all, playing the market, even though it is blackjack rather than pork bellies. Both are driven to play the game, be it the big casino on Wall Street or the little casinos of Tunica or Cherokee. The speculative stock market of the go-go eighties and the boom-boom nineties involved a lot of people, big and small, putting a lot of money in stocks (such as junk bonds or Internet stocks) where they hoped to make a lot of money very fast. Stocks are the functional equivalent of lottery tickets or betting slips, and you can beat the odds. Consult your psychic, bet the pot, and trust your luck. With this attitude, both investing and gambling are play, the sport of princes and paupers looking for something for nothing, a lot for a little, the big bundle. The distinction between millionaires investing in hedge funds and working stiffs betting on the horses or inside straights is nil.[15]

In the context of a society that views life as a game and every action—love, work, friendship, and now play—as a gamble, the metaphor has consequences. You bet your life because everything is for sale, every man has his price, and the winner is the one who ends up with the most toys. This pervasive attitude makes "the money game" more playful, but also makes the players more speculative and more reckless. When market values prevail, the winners at big gambles become cultural heroes, from mutual fund managers to lottery winners. But in all cases, the personal goal and the cultural heroism attached is to be able someday to afford to be nonproductive. The fantasy of big gambles with career, investment, or casino bets are the shimmering hope of self-expression: I am somebody by virtue of my success in acquisition, and hope to *really* be somebody by virtue of the acquired status of nonproductive play. The work ethic has given way to the play ethic when personal and economic risk is a matter of creating the conditions for entry into the leisure class. We are driven by the hope of becoming nondriven, of having the means to stop the world and get off. But first one has to play the game, hope for the main chance, take the big risk, and hope for the payoff. We may add that this motive spills over into crimes involving large amounts of money, from embezzling and fraud to robberies; in all cases, the hope appears to be a quick ride to easy street. A 1998 Charlotte, North Carolina, heist exemplifies this: a group of working-class folks of limited criminal experience managed to steal $17 million from Loomis Fargo bank transport service, but the "payoff" of quick riches became too much to resist. The lead couple immediately wanted the good life. They soon moved from a double-wide trailer into a $635,000 home, bought a BMW-Z3 automobile, a $43,000 diamond ring, and expensive antiques, placed in the new mansion along with a velvet Elvis painting and a wine cellar full of Pabst. These poor folks became a laughingstock, but in a way they are no different from many of the rest of us, who see getting rich quick at somebody else's expense as quite tempting; those who rig a deal to shaft their partners or talk a grandparent into writing their other relatives out of the will are no less motivated by the transcendent want for money above all other considerations. Pecuniary indecency is felt necessary for the accumulation of wealth as the means to self-expression, even if family and colleagues think you a crook and a jerk. The driven pursuit of wealth at great risk to reputation and even freedom signifies how much people invest their hopes in acquisition. In an entrepreneurial culture wherein big successes are celebrated, the great mass of lesser mortals are constantly shown images of the wealthy—in opulent settings at work and play, and with the creature comforts of an Ottoman pasha in their private pleasure domes. As avatars of the meaning of wealth, they remind us of what is widely believed: *the best enjoyment is expensive.* Or, more precisely, play still invites rankings: conspicuous and luxurious play beyond the reach of most people is deemed more desirable and pleasurable than ordinary play. And, since we are all now classified as entrepreneurs—managing our own fortune, guiding our own career, negotiating our own health insurance, and so on—we seek the levels and kinds of play we can afford, but also aspire to. If we can acquire the means, our enjoyment of play will tend upward toward the variants of play enjoyed at the top. This "Veblen effect" is familiar, but what is new is the urgency and expanse of the social principle of play. For youngish entrepreneurs, the desire to overspend on homes, cars, vacations, and so on that they can barely afford (and go into great debt to enjoy) is a compulsion born of aspiration: rather than keeping up with the Joneses, they desperately want to stay ahead of the Joneses. (In the 1990s, the personal savings rate of Americans was zero: we spent it all.) And the number of people involved in seeking vacation homes and tables at posh restaurants and in general "the best of everything expanded with the spread of new wealth." The difficulty is that exclusive play is by definition exclusive, so the aspiring many who seek access to Swiss ski resorts or New York restaurants or villas in Tuscany have competition for the sites of conspicuity. You may complain that your money is as good as anyone else's, but "being there" in the right places with the right people creates a crisis of competitive access to luxurious play. It remains the case that if everyone can and is doing it, it's not distinctive, and thus for the ambitious not worth doing. Currently, expensive play is becoming all the more exclusive. In places such as Aspen, the billionaires are forcing the millionaires out. Rather than go out to restaurants, the superrich hire famous chefs to cook for a dinner party at their place. For the status seekers, play remains an object of distinctiveness, something that is acquired along with all the other playthings of the good life. What is entertaining, however, is not the experience of play itself—they may find first night at the opera boring, hate skiing, and loathe French food—but rather the power to acquire it. In this regard, they are identical to the wretches who robbed Loomis Fargo and went on a buying spree: one uses wealth to have fun, and central to that fun is the delicious power to buy the upscale play you always wanted to have and now can. *It is fun to play even if it is defined as a commodity.*

LITE CULTURE

By the late twentieth century, the world was wired. Except for extremely remote places, one could telephone almost anywhere, as well as use faxes, e-mail, and even older media such as mail, ham radio, and telegraph. With cable television and radio, satellite dishes, and the Internet, great populations knew about events and processes in other places—who was cooperating or in conflict with whom, what was important at the moment, what was being read and seen and heard. Not only was there an interconnected world, but there was a world media elite. We refer here not only to those corporate powers who ran the world media institutions, but also to those visible people who were the celebrated beings of world mediation. We could know about, if we wished, those people who conducted the world's earnest efforts: politicians and bankers and corporate executives and interest groups. But we could also know about those people who conducted the world's play activities, or more precisely, came to represent the nature and direction of play for the rest of us to understand and often to emulate. There was not only the global reach of corporate and political power, but the power of a global popular culture, a culture of *play learning* that was superceding in importance the traditional institutions of learning.

The world entertainment economy obviously was by the mid-twentieth century the great purveyor of play culture. More people saw more movies than ever, consumed (one hesitates to say read) more books and magazines than ever, bought more music, traveled to more fun places, gambled more money, and in general engaged in more play than in any previous period in modern history. Despite the time crunch, people valued play so much that they found the time and money to have fun. For a growing segment of the population of many countries, play had become the primary social activity and even way of life. The culture of play had become so important to so many people that it was becoming the great growth industry and primary cultural activity of the world. The spirit of play was by now an ascendant attitude and habit that propagates the idea of cultural ludenics—whatever we do must be fun—in a wide variety of institutions and habits and with extensive global reach into places hitherto unaffected. We may be seeing a virtually universal urge to cultural lightness dramatized and propagated by mass mediation.

The omnipresence of media in our lives may be giving rise to a new kind of authority. Authority has traditionally been centered in either primary or secondary institutions, centered on sanguinary or contractual relations. Most people grow up in families in which authority is rooted in blood relations—parents, extended families, even tribes or clans. Sanguinary authority is the most ancient source of authoritative relations, wherein obedience is expected by appeal to familial or tribal relations. Contractual, or statutory, authority we associate with the rule of law, the state, and modern economic institutions: we are expected to obey on the basis of legal-rational criteria. In this case, the nation rather than the tribe became the typical political unit, and one obeyed the state because it was in our interest to do so. The "social contract" extended to work: rather than working in an extended family on a farm or craft, we worked for a business in which we contracted our labor for hire. Appeals to blood ties and appeals to contract ties still carry weight: "I owe it to my family" still compels people to obey, as an authoritative unit; "I signed a contract" obligates us to live up to what we agreed to. The socio-logic of blood being thicker than water, and that a deal is a deal, burdens us with the earnest duty to obey.

In the past hundred years or so, a new source of authority has arisen: rather than the primary authority of sanguine relations and the secondary authority of contractual relations, we now find authority in the tertiary authority of *mediational* relations. The media are thrice removed from our lives, unlike blood kin and primal ties, and work and associative relations such as politics, but media as an authority are removed from both our personal and associate lives, and influence us as an authoritative voice from afar. The newspaper came into people's lives in the late nineteenth century as "light reading," a brief mix of news, comics, gossip, weather, and so on. Soon it began to acquire a degree of authority: people found it a source not only of information, but of opinion. News was deemed a source of truth, and of conviction. Yet it was a disposable source of truth and lightly held convictions. Since news reading was play, what one learned from the newspaper was easily discarded or amended in subsequent days. The heavy beliefs about family and the state—group and national patriotism—were often reinforced by newspaper reading, but were given the aura of lightness by the popular flightiness and gaiety of the medium. The medium had its own metaphorical message:

we can tell you what's going on, and what opinions you should hold, but don't take us, or them, too seriously. News was an unenduring but ever-renewable commodity, an object of media play over the "news cycle" of the next edition or broadcast.

Perhaps the real importance of the pioneering probes of Marshall McLuhan was that he first saw clearly that we were entering an era of *media play*. Previous sources of authority had been closer and heavier; media authority derived from its very remoteness and lightness. A newspaper seemed to know what was going on everywhere and could say so with brevity and wit, and "opinion leaders" could give glib and usually emotive articulation as to what was "right thinking" on a subject at the moment. Both news and opinion could change quickly, so media people quickly learned that authoritative statements of fact and value were amendable. What was authoritative was what was up to date. Facts and opinions had the lightness of the temporary and transient medium that communicated them. In a world pervaded by media, authoritative messages become a feature of fleeting and fashionable style. News became a pleasure-giving medium, and the great majority of news readers sought it out as a playful authority. Media communications developed as a language to be played with and then discarded, an immediate and dispensable cavalcade of attention-getting messages and stories that are a perishable commodity.

In his own inimitable way, McLuhan understood that the proliferation of media had profound effects on the way we perceived the world, giving us new imaginative frames as the users, or "content," of media. Every medium has a structure and format in the way it communicates, and once established, that structure becomes a vehicle for ritual play with the medium. In many cultures, ritual play is often earnest and sacred ceremonial, such as the ecstatic Ghost Dance of the Plains Indians. But our contemporary mass media are both playful and profane, so the rituals take the form of audience-pleasing ceremonials. In a sense, we are media, since we dictate the formats and genres that become part of the repeatable and predictable vision of the world that, say, newspapers and TV programming give us. The daily newspaper developed *formulas* that structured our expectations as to ritual content—the human interest story, the celebrity gossip column, the sports page, the front page mix, and so on—which became familiar and entertaining. The play of mediated entertainment became the "ritual center" of modern culture.[16]

So the Information Age turns out to be the Entertainment Age. Information has to be entertaining, or it is not informative. Informa-

tion is something to play with. We do not seek knowledge that
requires painful effort, but rather knowledge that conveys playful
delights. McLuhan's children, namely all of us, have dictated that
the media communicate play. The metamessage of every medium,
oral, scriptorial, or visual, is that to be palatable to our ludenic
tastes, it must adhere to our prime criterion of amusement. Mass
media exist and develop because of our desire for the playful messages they bring into our lives, and we want play because it is crucial
to overcoming perhaps the basic existential problem of modernity:
boredom. If the extreme "high" of play is ecstasy, the extreme "low" of
earnestness is boredom. A good bit of work, daily routine, and "un-
filled" time involves a state of boredom, which may be the "represen-
tative modern state of mind," prompting the "resultant need for
distraction."[17] McLuhan hypothesized that media are "extensions of
man," even primitive tools such as the wheel and the hoe and shovel.
But it may also be that as media structures and institutions become
more sophisticated, they move from utilitarian to play functions.
Gardeners now use wheelbarrows and hoes for garden play rather
than subsistence agriculture. A glance at best-seller lists and a walk
through a franchise bookstore alerts us to the fate of "serious" literature (writers have become "content providers"). In order to keep a
medium from becoming boring, we as the users desire constant
changes or variations in the content, to the point that nothing can be
taken "straight." TV or movies or novels or even children's fare become parodic or satirical, self-referential and self-mocking. The mediational extensions of man wind up making much fun of us, their
creator.

Boredom is like the bleak "dark matter" that physicists think pervades the universe: it is a common and tedious dimension of contemporary existence. But in the media age, we no longer think that
boredom has to be endured or overcome by self-initiated action.
Rather, it can be relieved through media access. The antidote for the
dread experience of boredom is tuning in to some external source of
entertainment. This ranges from those working out at a health club
who require a Walkman while running or a TV monitor while on a
stationary bicycle, to those who constantly surf the 'Net or flip channels in search of some media site that will hold their attention. But
the difficulty with such felt necessity to be "connected" is that its
very inexhaustible availability eventually becomes boring. Even if
the forms and genres of popular mediation are repetitious variations
on themes, we want them as an expectation that boredom can be
"cured" by filling time with media fare. The desperate hope for grati-

fication leads us to scan and fixate on external forms of entertainment. Play must be provided for the bored, who appear to be both hungry for and jaded by experience, at once fearful of periods of quiet that might invite reflection or creativity and drawn to the familiar and ritualized forms of media experience—the game show, the talk show, the news show—as a narcotic that satisfies through scripted media play. (The improvised and spontaneous are largely eliminated in formulaic media ceremonials.)

With media play, boredom is relieved by vicarious attention to a medium. Any medium of communication—a comic book, a novel, a TV show, a video game—must combine familiarity and novelty. The format of a TV show should conform to the structure of the television medium, fitting our expectations about visuality, media time, and media traditions, but also introduce a modicum of novelty that makes it a variation on media themes but offers something new and fashionable into the formulaic content of the medium. New media fare comes out of the familiar "ground" of the medium—habits and frames of reference—and are expressed in the new "figures"—plots and metaphors, phrases and images, icons and idols, spectacles and shows—that appeal to our vicarious thirst for novelty. In that way a medium holds our attention, making us comfortable by the familiarity of form and interested by the newness of content. Media play satisfies our want for stimulating and exciting experience, made palatable as imaginative if noninvolving participation. This insatiable desire affects all mediums: *the demand for play tends to drive serious media formats and messages out in favor of lighter and more frivolous fare.* If we media people do indeed ultimately dictate the form and content of mediation, then our existential impulse and historic trend is toward the expansion of enjoyment of ludenic pleasantries defined as fun. Despite what earnest cultural critics decry as tasteless, debasing, and indecent, in our use of the media, we insist on having what we call a good time.

The social demand for media play, then, is irresistible and cumulative. The popular curriculum of all widespread and accessible media tends toward featuring play experiences. The serious novel is superceded by the wide array of popular paperbacks. Newspapers revamp their format to appeal by running lighter fare—human interest stories, sports, home features, lots of pictures of wrecks and beautiful people, and local and humorous fare. News as an enterprise tends toward the tabloid, with formerly magisterial organizations such as CBS, the BBC, and the *Washington Post* sensationalizing their news product, at least following the lead of popular news outlets that define the lowest common denominators as to what is important news: rumors of presidential fellatio, tales of palace intrigues, features on celebrity activists, exposés of scams and fleecings, and so forth. The journalistic account evolves into a "news show" that becomes a carnival sideshow. The serious and highbrow fare TV networks used to run—operas, serious dramas, news analyses, educational programs, and the like—have vanished. All media moguls learn the lesson that media play is profitable, and that they are increasingly in the business of selling entertainment. The modal media person is essentially a voyeur, whose desire for imaginative participation does not exclude the tasteless and sensate, and who puts a premium on the satisfaction of prurient interest. For media people, looking with curiosity is playing, with the world characterized and observed as one gigantic peep show.

The media player defines everything as within the purview of enjoyable witness, and media providers are in the position of competing for display of those messages that appeal to the desire to know about everything previously forbidden as taboo, lurid, or private. To compete in the play world, the media invite and encourage us to look without shame, justified by the excuse that it is, after all, only in fun. We can observe anything we want as long as we don't do it seriously. We want to see things that are fun to watch. Instead of justification by faith, we now have justification by play.

The voyeur model of media experience is reminiscent of Tertullian, the Christian church father who maintained (in *De Spectaculis*, ca.198 A.D.) that one of the joys of heaven will be that the pious elect, who abjured earthly pleasures, can observe the torments of the damned through a kind of window on hell. Tertullian noted that the saved remnant does not have to recoil in horror or in sadness from this spectacle; quite the contrary, the heavenly host are supposed to enjoy it ("marvel, laugh, rejoice, and exult"). One of the redemptive rewards of salvation is to watch with smug glee the endless suffering of those condemned to eternal perdition. Heavenly play includes the observation of the earnest wrath of God toward those who had earthly and sinful fun on Earth.[18]

Today the *Tertullian invitation* continues in the media age: we the media patrons want to observe, from the distanced safety of mediation, the full range of human woe. The Tertullians of popular news and programming invite us to become legitimate voyeurs, viewing their exhibition of sin and suffering, idiocy and criminality, failure and disaster, the various fates of human angels, demons, and vermin. For media voyeurs, the world is characterized as a dreadful and random but forever fascinating place. Nature foments disasters, man's inhumanity to man is rampant, accidents and mistakes wreak havoc, the best-laid and biggest schemes go awry (call it "Titanic irony"), and authority is weak and self-serving and untrustworthy. Popular media—tabloids, reality-based programming, TV and radio evangelists, demagogic pundits—so portray a hopelessly dangerous and frightening world that it gives credence to apocalyptic and paranoid fantasies. People love it. The media voyeur seeks covert observation of scandalous or disastrous spectacles for the sheer joy of witnessing secondhand a variety of unguilty pleasures: hot pursuits, dangerous rescues, twisters, earthquakes, hurricanes, executions, celebrities off-guard, crashes, royal weddings and funerals, politicians' gaffes and clumsiness, nudity, combat, and so on. War has become a spectator sport, a conflict to be observed as sort of the ultimate reality-based program. Like the Peeping Tom, the media voyeur is taken with the social pathology of scopophilia, only multiplied and legitimated by media organizations who cater to our widespread desire for vicarious media play, no matter how intrusive or vulgar. (There are even Web sites where one can watch the very private lives of people who have volunteered to be watched continuously, including their bathroom and bedroom functions.) Tertullian's denizens of hell have been expanded to include everyone who can be watched. The heaven of media access turns all the rest of us into watchers who observe life through popular mediation rather than live life through participation. Once we lived life; now we observe other people's lives.

The desire for voyeuristic experience through media access to the private expands what is legitimate to know and see. People from presidents to paupers may protest that they have private lives, but this does little to quell the demand for knowing everything about them. We are sure that everyone great and small is not only noteworthy but notorious, and that social worth is contradicted by private notoriety. Since all things are fraudulent, it is legitimate to inquire about and inspect all claims to worth. This makes society *transparent*, and everyone subject to both legal and mediational inquiry to find out the awful yet delightful truth. Yet often enough voyeuristic media play is transactional: the observed usually enjoy being watched, and willingly bare all. Some celebrities make transparency into a part of their publicity campaign to advertise themselves, and are emulated by so many who seek some brief moment of celebrity that they are willing to be known and seen in their entirety. McLuhan's "global village" includes the nosiness of the mythical village of old, only now it is not that everyone has something to hide but rather that everyone has something they want exposed. In the old village, exposure meant shame and loss of private reputation; in the global village, exposure means fame and gain of public reputation.

Society is now not only transparent, it is *flippant*. We think that we can and should see through everything and everyone, but also that we owe nothing or no one proper respect or seriousness. By seeking immediate and titillating experience, we trivialize all values and are impertinent about all claims to authority or tradition. This tends to make social relations transient and noncommittal, and events previously designated as serious or somber now viewed as comic or ironic. Shocking events (such as the *Challenger* explosion or the death of Princess Diana) produce sorrow in some, but also an immediate outpouring of jokes. The flippant help create a "flip" culture they can pick and choose (armed with their TV remote, the "flipper," scanning channels and quickly rejecting discordant or weighty messages). We learn flippancy from many sources, including the media: note how popular news recounts events such as the doings of a presidential candidate. The candidate is often portrayed as a minor comic figure in a corrupt melodrama, saying trivial things that are boring and meaningless. The candidate is a play-figure at whom we may sneer, since we've heard it all before and since, after all, she or he is a fraud. The "newsperson's smirk" communicates winking complicity in the attitude of glib dismissal of aspirations to be taken seriously. The flippant know better, and accord little regard for anything deemed important; all seriosity is dissonant, and reduced to a minor key that may be safely ignored.

Finally, society is also by now what we may term *easy*. The attitude of playfulness gives credence to regarding choices and values as easy, taking things at ease, and attempting to remain as careless and unexacting as possible. People would rather be pleasant than smart, carefree than careworn, facile than reflective. Making "hard" choices or imposing a regime of severity are avoided. The air of ease dictates soft choices entered into lightly, and the preference for a life of comfort and painlessness. Religious conversion seems to be a soft choice that many people enter into but from which they easily "backslide"; religiosity is comfortable and avoids the agony of faith. Even something as simple as dieting is at odds with the principle of social ease: eating is play, and the pleasure of good food can lead to obesity (most Americans are overweight), but dieting involves the discomfort of denial. It is no wonder that a massive dietary industry exists promising easy ways to lose weight, or that you can eat what you want without gaining weight. Indulgence without consequence is a core feature of the play world. Similarly, media news is now structured to ease us into the program. We may experience news without involvement, since the news industry and we are implicitly merely "eyewitnesses" to events for which we have no responsibility: accidents, wars, child abuse, crime, and so on. Bad news is countered with good news, interspersed with jocularity about the weather, light fare such as sports and features, and much happy talk. We may indulge in the news without taking it seriously. The lite culture puts a high premium on easiness. When someone is described as "easy to get along with," this is a compliment; when someone says of themselves, "I'm easy," that is an advertisement for an agreeable self; when a girl or boy is designated as "easy," this means they are willing to engage in pleasurable (often sexual) intercourse. The easy manner—natural, unaffected, friendly, smooth, and unconcerned—is much cultivated by celebrities, politicians, and propagandists. We may suggest that transparency, flippancy, and easiness are integral parts of our contemporary mind, self, and society. The lite culture of play is quite like lite beer or the myriad of objects marketed as without weight: the emphasis is placed on immediate exhibition, uninvolving levity, and quick flightiness.

If all this sounds like a description of a *carnival culture*, that's because it is. We wish the media at our disposal to transport us to the frivolities and indelicacies of the carnival. We want to walk down the bright and loud midway and see the gaudy variety and festive gaiety of the media carnival. We like to hear the barkers make their pitch, see the teasers on the stages luring us inside, play the games where we are sure to win a prize. We wish for the media carnival to bring us new *enchantment*, just like the traveling circuses and troubadours and magicians of old. We yearn to see dazzling acts, hear tales of the great and remote and bizarre, experience the magic absent in the earnest monotony of our lives. The media carnival brings light into our lives, makes light of all that we take too seriously, lightens the burdens of the day. Media play illuminates our world, and enchants us with the luminous. In the *ludi publici* of our carnival culture, we the *homo ludens* of today fondly hope that the lights will never go out and that the music always plays.

LET'S CELEBRATE!

The enchantments of the carnival culture can best be thought of as an unending series and field of *celebrations*. If it is the case that every form of popular mediation tends toward the representation of play, then what is read and seen and heard and spoken today becomes a ludenic celebration of cultural symbols, our "essential life" given festive and vivid dramatic form. Media celebrations show us "a world that is a projection of the ideals created by the community," allowing us to vicariously join "a world of contending forces as an observer at play." These social symbols (not necessarily limited to "ideals") are major motifs recurrent in our popular media, and may be taken as dramatic projections that we media people like to observe at play. We like to see mediated celebrations of people who represent these symbols, both positively and negatively. A positive celebration accords ceremonial honor to the one celebrated. A negative celebration, a media variant of the "degradation ceremony," dishonors those under scrutiny by lowering their status or reputation. We celebrate saints and sinners, enjoying them as media objects of play who exist for us as amusements that pleasure or displeasure us according to our mood and whim. Media players are a fickle lot, so who is honored and who is dishonored can change very quickly, as can who is in the spotlight and who vanishes. Like the agitated crowds at Roman gladiatorial matches, we are quick to vote thumbs up or thumbs down.[19]

Some media celebrations are obvious, others not: our friend Veblen alerted us earlier to the visible social drama of displayed wealth, and the *celebration of wealth* continues to be a powerful ideal, both as a positive ("Wealth is good") and negative ("Wealth is evil") symbol. Movie and TV dramas in opulent settings are advertisements for the high good life, and gossip magazines focusing on the rich (such as *Vanity Fair*) depict their personal and financial messes but also their privilege and pursuit of expensive pleasures. The legitimacy of opulent consumption continues to be a major pitch in advertising, making the association of magical allure with a product or service that gives the consumer the power to acquire and enjoy attractive qualities or experiences. With the proliferation of the financial media industry (magazines such as *Forbes* and *Fortune*, financial channels such as CNBC and CNN/FN), corporate moguls and financial wizards have acquired new and soaring celebrity currency in the marketplace of fame. Whereas once they would have been "captains of industry," now they tend to be corporate raiders and mutual fund managers and financial manipulators. Rather than idols of production or even consumption, now they tend to be regaled as *idols of accumulation*. The media interest focuses on how much they are worth, how they plan to acquire more, and what kind of status this entitles them to. In a winner-take-all economy, we are interested to know who the leaders of the capitalist pack are, and what we can do to emulate their staggering success. Further, the economic reportage industry serves a propaganda function, celebrating not only the success of giants of accumulation, but the idea of accumulation itself. The metamessage of *The Wall Street Journal* and CNBC is, "Gain is good and goes to the best and brightest," and here they are, the idols of accumulation; here's what they've got, and how richly they live. The typical profile displays their opulent surrounds and power of privilege: they have the means to choose to play if it is their will. These celebrations contain no hint of *illth*, or the disease of kleptomanic "affluenza"; the successful are portrayed as happy with the weal of their success, content in their Edenic existence in multiple homes and private jets and stretch limos and all the accumulations of Veblen's "pure display." Negatively, however, other media (tabloids, for instance, with their populist and lower-class appeal) portray the rich as an undeserving and extravagant lot, who came by their wealth through inheritance, luck, or crime and lead a life of decadence and wretched excess on loot taken from the commonwealth. A whole genre of popular stories portrays in lurid detail the foibles and conceits of those cursed with riches, which we the unrich may follow with glee, enjoying the self-induced torment and degradation of the undeserving rich. Both images taken together suggest our abiding ambivalence about those who are different by having more money, an attitude combining or alternating admiration and contempt. But we certainly enjoy playing with popular images of the rich, those idols of modern Mammon who represent for us the idolatry and allure of the marketplace.

Another representation of media play is the celebration of the celebrated, those known for being well known, depicting the ascendant *idols of renown*. We both admire and revile those who seek and find acclaim, and enjoy depictions of their play-lives. Like the rich, the famous are figures of ludenic style. Popular audiences enjoy their display of their public selves, in their parades of sartorial exposure at awards events or other occasions of self-display. The celebrity is a creature of narcissistic exhibitionism, fascinating to us, the unrenowned, for their lack of modesty or shame and their willingness to be observed. The affectation of the renowned is a source of considerable play experience, from sexual fantasies about alluring stars to amusement at their wretched excesses. Their demand for special treatment—perquisites and privileges—validates their status as popular royalty who occupy momentarily the grand procession of fame, but also disgust us by their arrogant self-assertion as new gods. So we relish their moment of fame, but also enjoy their eclipse and even disappearance. Whether we regard them with admiration or contempt, we exercise the ultimate power over them. If we do not consider them worthy of our vicarious play, the light we shine on them goes out and they fade out of sight. If we do not see them, they are not there. As figures of fashion, these idols of renown vanish like ghosts when they no longer amuse us.

Similarly, figures of power may occupy positions of authority and direction, but in the popular mind they often are regarded as *idols of domination*. Other figures may have fame or wealth, but these have might, and people are as drawn to figures of power as they are to figures of renown or accumulation. The popular royalty of politics and war are idolized not only as leaders, but because they possess great power, which connotes to many a special aura of potency. Their dominative qualities make them attractive to some, repellent to others. But in both attitudes the popular tendency again is to regard them as figures of play. We enjoy both their triumphs and their pratfalls, and often regard them with amused contempt. Others imbue them with charismatic powers, and consider themselves blessed to be touched or noticed by them. Women who sought the sexual favors of the seven original astronauts, various political candidates, war heroes, and presidents are only the most egregious example of fantasies reducing domination to the erotic, the political becoming the personal.

In all these cases, we see that the wealthy, the famous, and the powerful are made into idols, but they are not universally venerated as figures of grandeur. Our stance toward them may depend upon how much we envy or despise idols created by kleptomania, exhibitionism, or megalomania. In any case, the contemporary attitude tends to regard them lightly. Rather than threats, they are popular play-figures, toys of our imagination over whom we enjoy feeling morally superior. Even though their social weight is heavy, we regard them lightly through making light of them. They are little more than fictions to us, and despite their superior rank, we usually consider them lightweights who are prisoners of their money, their desperate quest for fame, or their power. They exist for us as creatures of play: *we expect for them to have fun, and for us to have fun with them.* The rich, the famous, and the powerful become objects of derision if they are serious, shy, and humorless. The very wealthy have begun to hire publicists who help groom their public image to make them appear fairly normal, able to have fun and take a joke, and communicate with ordinary folks. A celebrity who jealously guards his or her private life is deemed strange, since the celebrated are expected to bare all. And it is the kiss of death for politicians if they are too earnest or too obviously power hungry: presidential politicos afflicted with terminal seriosity such as Jimmy Carter, Michael Dukakis, and John McCain were altogether too heavy, and Richard Nixon's will to power was much too obvious. Like anyone who conveys seriosity, they were constantly told by their advisers to "lighten up." Successful pols such as Ronald Reagan and Bill Clinton hired joke writers, excelled at public emotion, and as celebrities endured the intrusive and embarrassing invasion of their private lives, in the former case the less than perfect family and in the latter the less than perfect husband.

By century's end, perhaps the primary form of critical discourse was no longer the serious book or essay or newspaper column or public speech but rather the satire. Since people appeared no longer to respect or defer to important public figures, they became fair game for satirists. Caricature still distorted the features of public figures, but they were usually not portrayed as sinister or conspiratorial or mean as much as they were preposterous. In the spirit of Veblen, the wealthy were the stuff of parodic derision, pathetic creatures more to be pitied than feared. Celebrities were burlesqued as flaming egotists, most of whom had achieved fame without the burden of talent. Politicians tended to be caricatured as buffoons always inadequate to master situations; the exercise of power was ridiculed even in the most serious of situations, such as war or natural catastrophe. The news joined in the fun: cultural news that covered celebrities set the style of snide and derisive banter about the famous, who were almost uniformly portrayed as foolish; political news acquired an air of mirth, and by the 1990s it was common for political reporting and commentary to portray politicians in mocking and sarcastic terms, and to display ironic contempt for their subject, politics. Economic reporters were more deferential, but when the great bull market ends and economic difficulty returns, we may expect them to lampoon the fools of Wall Street as pied pipers whom we foolishly trusted. (A variant on this form of ridicule was the bevy of former employees of the great, such as presidential aides Donald Regan and George Stephanopolous, who wrote embarrassing exposés of their former bosses, proving that the price of humorous exposure is higher than dignified appraisal.)

This playful attitude toward the high and mighty suggests an ambivalence, since we seem to be at once envious and iconoclastic. We both want to be like them, and at the same time enjoy seeing them fail or falter. This lets us have our play both ways: we can admire and emulate the great, but also "democratize" them by degrading them. Recall that rituals of celebration are complemented by degradation ceremonies, in which we lower the status of our mediated play-figures. This does not mean we want them punished or banished; on the contrary, they are so important to us that we want the great media parade of fools to continue as long as they keep us laughing. The function of social elites in the play world is quite different than before: we can tolerate their special status as rich, famous, or powerful as long as they remain figures of fun. We allow them their wealth and renown and power only if we don't have to take them too seriously. Our envy or distaste for them is mitigated by disallowing them heroic or even villainous qualities. They can keep their money or prestige or might if we are allowed to consider them fools.

The principle of playful entertainment also applies to other kinds of idols and idolatry. Many of us idolize, with the same ambivalence, those who come to represent ability at social expression, social rebellion, or social sensuality. *Idols of social expression* include all those who become celebrated for their ability to articulate popular sentiments or provoke popular delight, especially through use of the media of mass communication. The truly great communicators of the twentieth century have been those who could translate media messages into play. They became known, and admired or reviled, as messengers of playful communications. The history of news, for instance, is replete with the triumph of the rhetoric of popular play over elite seriosity. The Pulitzers and Hearsts made news reading into fun, and the moguls of Hollywood and TV networks made news into entertaining newsreels and news shows. News commentary centered on the "op-ed" column by a prestigious elite figure such as Walter Lippmann. But this was countered by such figures as the pioneering Walter Winchell, who made himself into a celebrity by his streetwise banter, first in his syndicated column and then on the radio. With his characteristic gossipy and staccato treatment of news, he established the expressive habit that all are equal, and revealed, in the drumbeat of news. "You call it schmooze, I say it's news," said Winchell; his intuitive understanding was that news is not newsworthy unless it induces a state of play in the news-consuming populace. The media descendants of Winchell are today's talk radio hosts and celebrity pundits who are glib, gossipy, and see scandal as the primary subject of news. Their skill at mediated expression is predicated on the populist sense that we do not connect "deep to deep" but rather "beep to beep." The principle of playful media expression also applies to successful communicators of weather, financial news, cooking, and so on. For those who prefer that news be straight and serious, or that opinionated talk be conducted with courtesy and decorum, the contemporary news scene appears dreadful. Punditry and news talk cater to our electronic itch for gossip conducted by those versed in the arts of expressing malice. News rhetoric has acquired the habit of assuming that society and individuals are transparencies to be examined and found wanting, that an air of flippancy is a cool news attitude, and that news can move quietly from one subject to another with casual and cynical ease. And the more democratic forums, such as call-in shows and Internet chat rooms, although less articulate, certainly seem more ardent. The developing democracy of expression should remind us that in an age of ubiquitous mediation, everyone may be getting on everyone else's nerves, because in McLuhanesque terms, we *are* each other's nerves. By extension, the metamessage of news is that society is funny because it is thoroughly corrupt and unredeemable, something that can be understood only through the ironic and knowing model of reportage and the light touch of news formats.[20]

We are drawn to *idols of rebellion* because they take a critical stance against society a step further, to the point of actual disobedience or contempt for the extant order. Like media voyeurism, admiration for rebel figures can stem from quite pathological urges, such as the astounding persistence of often covert admiration for certifiable fiends such as Hitler or ruthless criminals such as Mafia dons or con artists. But most people seem to be amused by milder rebellious figures given media exposure as an alternative to normal and mundane life. Rock stars who smash equipment and trash hotel rooms, movie stars who "act up," or political activists who make a nuisance of themselves give us pleasure through news of their public antics. It is clear that we restrict our own rebellions largely to style, by wearing the clothes or using the languages of rebellion, and by occasional covert acts such as smoking marijuana or rooting for a prominent rebel. "Hip consumerism" has become an important feature of advertising and marketing, appealing to pseudorebels who restricted rebellion to consuming products identified with insurgence or nonconformity. Media industries such as music and movies find ever renewed ways to package mediated rebellion, with new singers or actors who exemplify the latest stylistic forms of cultural antiestablishmentarianism. On television, some forms of ritual rebellion endure, such as professional wrestling. Wrestling is patently phony, to be sure, but many enjoy watching the ritualized parody of violence that satirizes social divisions and the absurdity of conflict. The earnest effort and anxious conflict of media sports are transformed into ceremonial play, wherein violence is not so much a tactic as an art form. The colorful rebels of "rasslin" are enjoyable as comic figures who both allow us to follow the prescribed drama of the match and let us in on its fundamental fraudulence. That way we can enjoy both the rebels of the show and what a joke the show itself is. This is a play attitude that applies to many other areas of life, and helps explain why figures from show business (including a former wrestler who became a state governor) have succeeded in bringing those values into "real life." Ronald Reagan, after all, billed himself as a "citizen politician" who was a rebel against the system, and as president, left office damning the government he had headed for eight years.

The same sort of fantasy life compels our interest in *idols of sensuality*. There is evidence that the sexual life of most people is pretty tame and fairly infrequent. Since an active and varied sexual life involves social risks similar to overt rebellions, a good bit of our contemporary carnal life is mediated, ranging from watching advertisements to pornographic movies. We are enormous consumers of, if not always active participants in, sexuality. In so doing, we project fantasies on sensual idols, those who are desirable and those who claim to fulfill desires. The desirable are observable in a variety of venues, from fashion shows to centerfolds to music videos. Those who appeal to a current norm of beauty can be elevated to the status of an idol of attractiveness. We celebrate their sensual appeal, but like the unattainable women and men of medieval romance, they exist in a court of love beyond our reach. But they become the luscious forms of our daydreams, those idealized gods of pleasure with whom we can imagine ourselves gamboling in ecstatic sexual play in some dewy elysian field of golden sunlight.

Media figures are all objects of momentary amusement rather than emulation. A talk radio host, celebrated rebel movie star, or supermodel are playthings who exist only for our diversion and not edification. They function for us less as role models than as ludenic toys who live in the noncorporeal space of media ether. They are players in what McLuhan called our *discarnate* lives. We are voyeurs of media expression, rebellion, and sensual display, observing selected play-figures who live in an ethereal realm beyond our quotidian existence. Discarnate beings are creations of media magic, and their meaning for us is magical. Idols can use magic, conjuring up wealth, fame, and power we can only imagine, or representing acts of expression, rebellion, or sensuality we can only observe mediated from afar.

Because of this discarnate distance, we have been relegated to the role of audience looking curiously at unreal things. We understand them as belonging to a realm we cannot ever enter nor fully understand, and tend not to take them seriously. From politicians to centerfolds, we think of them as comic idols, less than Olympian but more than mere mortals. There is for us something inherently funny about the media cavalcade of popular idols, whom we celebrate as ludenic, and very perishable, gods. They are fun, but we are aware that they live somewhere else.

Those who grew up in modern societies in the latter half of the twentieth century are well aware of the media's role in expanding the field of the risible. As cultural selectivity became more divergent, young people developed the habit of seeking and finding ludenic pleasures and excitements. When the youth culture became more powerful as a social harbinger, this new force brought a lifetime of learning from popular culture that it is legitimate to have fun. Children's programming, comic books, cartoons, Disney movies, motion pictures, and so forth included one powerful metamessage: all these wonderful diversions themselves tell us that play is more fun than any other kind of activity. Children might watch highly moral or edifying fare provided by institutional authorities, Biblical movies, and school assemblies that couch a message of social importance (Don't take drugs, abstain from sex, study hard) in a convivial program. The moral imperative is usually either forgotten or readily agreed to, but what is truly conveyed is, "That was fun." By the logic of fun morality, young people learned that premise and what follows: since that was fun, why don't I seek more experiences that are as much fun, or even more? The introduction of fun experiences into serious institutions undermines the attitude of earnest seriosity. As students became more and more enamored of mediated and noninstitutional fun, institutions thought the incorporation of fun would make institutional learning more palatable. In fact, what it did was whet young people's interest in fun. The movie show at school, the music performed at church, the example of the swinging bachelor uncle or aunt who shows up at a family reunion with tales of Parisian parties—all these impress the young person with the possibility of fun as an alternative to the routines of life.

By the 1960s, youth in Western countries were thoroughly immersed in a *culture of fun*. To be sure, they were told by adult authorities of their social responsibilities and moral obligations. But social conditions had changed. The social responsibility to be a soldier, parent, family member, or even employed worker had lessened; moral strictures changed in the wake of the pleasure principle enunciated by advertising, the availability of birth control, the gift of widespread good health, and the mobility provided by the automobile. All these factors helped define the period of youthfulness as "the time of your life," a time to ignore or postpone serious adulthood to have fun. So a romantic and hedonistic culture developed around the "baby boomers" in various lands. Since this culture was "ours," it was an *alternative* culture counter to the official institutional arrangements. Youth sought their own celebratory music, formed egalitarian peer groups, became mobile and experimental, identified with bohemian and artistic values and lifestyles. Their idols were alternative gods to the official ones, often new idols of expression, rebellion, and sensuality—the Beatles and the Doors, artists and poets such as James Dean and Jack Kerouac, revolutionaries such as Che Guevara, sexual gurus such as Hugh Hefner and Helen Gurley Brown, visionaries such as Timothy Leary and Norman O. Brown. (It should also be noted that John F. Kennedy became the model for a fun president—humorous, relaxed, able to have fun, communicating an aura of youthful sensuality that was later verified to be quite vigorous.) But the dynamic of the cultural upheaval of the sixties and beyond was the principle of fun applied to the new culture: express yourself by telling it like it is, rebel against the staid and stodgy and uptight by doing your own thing, and enjoy the body electric by balling and toking and rocking. The values of the counterculture were ludenic values, committed at base to individual pleasures from which derived the dynamic of social reform. The "party of eros" that emerged during that period gave philosophical justification to expressive, rebellious, and erotic adventures as a cathartic probe toward individual and social liberation.[21] *If society would just have more fun, there would be less evil in the world.* (It is no accident that the "movement" of the sixties began to run into trouble when it began to take itself too seriously; when the focus changed from the lively expansion of fun to the dreary articulation of a political agenda, it lost adherents and allies who admired its vivacity but disliked its pretensions.)

Since the injunction to have fun was already overtly pervasive in advertising and latent in prosperity, there is a sense in which society quickly and easily took them up on the challenge. The values and styles associated with youthful leisure diffused upward to older and established people, and the ethos of fun became ingrained in bourgeois habits. Youthful fun became a central motif of fashion, communicating to society at large the value of self-expression, stylistic rebellions, and sensual indulgence, even if they have been tamed down to contributing to political charities, wearing leisurely clothes, and buying erotic lingerie. The ethos of fun-loving evolved into a social norm: those who are serious-minded or earnest-spoken are regarded as wearying bores and mind-numbing drones. The accusation "You're no fun" became important, since it attached the stigma of *gravitas* and solemnity to someone; inability to "lighten up," take and tell a joke, relax and "kick back," and the refusal to have fun became regarded as symptoms of a major character flaw. *If you are not playful and don't know how to have fun, there is something wrong with you.* You become the subject of envy if you have a "fun job"; an enviable couple is a "fun couple"; those hard at work envy a coworker or friend who is enjoying a respite at some "fun place"; a convivial gathering of friends is recalled as a "fun time." *The world is supposed to be a fun place, and the best people in it are fun people.*

A fun person is someone who is playful, appears cheerful and vigorous and animated, knows how to have fun, and inheres individual and social meaning to play. In late twentieth-century societies, a major character motif, even a modal personality, is guilt-free playfulness, the characteristic attitude of carefree lightness and bearing of personal radiance. Lightheartedness and even light-headedness are primary virtues, contrasted with heavier virtues of past times such as zeal and intelligence. (In America, it is interesting to note that among those important social figures who rejected the sixties, many in fact became identified with easy relaxation and flippant unintelligence, such as Ronald Reagan; intelligent zealots who hate and blame the sixties, such as William Bennett and Robert Bork, are regarded as unfunny spoilsports and heavy bores.) People of various political and social views all are judged by the *criterion of play*: are they someone able to have fun, tolerate fun, and promote fun? Presidents and prime ministers, with the Kennedy and Reagan precedents, are at least portrayed as having a fun life, able to relax and enjoy leisure, as people persons who are warm and personable, who enjoin those around them to play, and most importantly, do not interfere with and indeed promote by example and policy the burgeoning culture of play. A social leader outside of groups committed either to zealotry (such as Christian Right groups) or to intelligence (such as academic organizations) must display signs of being a fun person to be fully trusted. If this attitude adds up to a social vision, it is that playful people have become both a personal ideal and a cultural norm, and that our imagination of society is moving from focus on graven images toward ludenic images. Society at its best should not be a serious and somber place, but rather should commit to being more playful and allowing people to have more fun.

The same process may be noted in contemporary organizations. It is common in popular culture to portray traditional institutions as stolid and altogether too solemn, something enlivened by fun people. The army, the corporation, the White House or Congress, the university—all are subject to being "trashed" and revitalized by the intrusion of people whose playful attitude shakes up earnest and oh-so-serious things. The "funny people," in the spirit of the sixties, don't accept the earnest premises of the organization, and their antics impose chaos on order. (In modern popular culture, this approach to organizational life is perhaps best exemplified by the Marx Brothers.) This popular motif has a moral: organizations are so overearnest and self-important that they require puckish figures to expose their solemnity. In the popular mind, *organized seriosity is a joke, something that evokes comic treatment and arouses amusement.* In response, real organizations often try to accommodate this dislike of seriosity by adjustments that make work, worship, or whatever less dreary or grave. A congenial workplace ranks at the top of what people want out of work, and a considerable literature exists recommending how to make the working environment less threatening and indeed more fun. (Corporations now experiment with day care at the office, and occasions where the older children come to work with Daddy or Mommy; the mere presence of kids who have not lost the capacity to have fun, and are puzzled by why so much work is going on here, may have serendipitous effects on the conduct of effort.) The same ludenic appeal has been adopted by some church organizations, since many people have memories of the grim organized seriosity of church services. (A flyer appealing for a local church announces a changing church: "If you feel . . . people should be friendly and show it/music should be contemporary and upbeat/casual dress is OK/messages should be positive, practical, relate to my daily life/children should enjoy church and not dread it/who I am is more important than what I've got"; the religious experience of worship is described as "fun," "exciting," "dynamic," with a "children's action-packed adventure land" and "small groups for intimacy, fellowship, and relationships" at a "contemporary church with the answers that will bring purpose, stability, and meaning to your life." All these messages convey the ethos of a fun place, wherein secular play rather than sacral piety becomes the appeal, and with slight alteration could easily be the pitch for a theme park or social fraternity.)

The lite culture of play, then, affects every individual and institution by the introduction of ludenic values into characterological and sociological patterns of culture. If being thought of as a "fun person" becomes critical to social acceptance, then the value of playfulness is incorporated into what one tries to be. (The much caricatured young women and girls of beauty contests attempt to convey this by appearing sprightly and effervescent, often to ludicrous excess, since they are expected to seem at once erotic and virginal.) Similarly, the intrusion of ludenic values into institutions previously deemed exclusively serious makes for considerable tensions, resistance, and organizational adaptation. This is no more evident in the present than in the conduct of school.

THE SCHOOL PLAY

Recall our image of the nineteenth-century school. Many older Americans even now remember school as a daily regimen, with largely rote learning of reading, writing, and arithmetic, and with discipline enforced by corporal punishment and public humiliation. Attendance was mandatory, and truant officers came after absent children. There was recess, and some extracurricular activities such as forensics and sports, but most learning was either "lessons" or patriotic and Biblical drill. School was a serious institution that made children into adults. Higher education had more ancillary activities that were fun (such as fraternities and sororities), but the thrust of college life was educative in the strict sense. At all levels, school was oriented toward production: producing students who learned knowledge and skills at a specified level for their productive entry into society. With the advent of modernity and industrialism, they increasingly were modeled on a factory, with all the techniques and skills necessary to manufacture educated adults. School as the first half of the twentieth century knew it was an artifact of the Machine Age, which was pervaded by a concern for the production of desired results. The means of education became the province of professionals—the "education industry"—who concentrated on *educational technique*, the search for ever more efficient ways to deliver the product, the certifiably educated student. The ends of education were usually confined to "basics," and most people did not go particularly deep into subjects or far in cumulative education (until about 1950, the United States, as well as other Western countries, graduated less than half of student-age people from high school).

The second half of the twentieth century witnessed an expansionary and curricular revolution in education. Here and abroad, school was broadened to include women and minorities, and was expected to educate a large segment of the population well into higher education. The demands on school at all levels became greater. The educational system was redesigned to introduce many more people, often with meager learning and motivation, to the intricacies of calculus and chemistry and statistics. Schools were expected to go beyond their traditional limited function for therapeutic tasks: teaching the uneducated and uneducable how to learn, dealing with social problems of race and gender and so on, counseling students with psychic difficulties, serving as employment agency, marital counselor, and on and on endlessly. This expansion of function obviously placed new burdens on school, and it performed these new tasks unevenly, but the wonder is, like the dog walking on its hind legs, not that it is done well but that it is done at all. By the end of the twentieth century, many countries had enormous sums and vast resources invested in school as a social institution, with the hope that educators could manage the great changes under way and still manage to produce useful and good adults able to function in the new economy and culture.

These demands on school obviously filtered down to the students, who became acutely aware that they were expected to perform. Technique dictated, for instance, a great expanse of testing, and quite naturally under external political and community pressure, teachers taught for the test. The student performance principle became the educational establishment's criterion for learning as measured by scores, and if students performed at appropriate levels, they were rewarded with credentials, proof that they were a worthy product. The difficulty and tension became important when students became consumers of school. Since they were expected to be consumers of everything else, it made sense to them that school was something to be critically evaluated like every other product. And since products were judged by the criterion of play, school could be evaluated by the same standard: Is it any fun? If not, why not? What can we do to make it more fun?

The counterpressure on school, then, has come from the consumers of education, and they exercise great if subtle power as to what goes on there. The powers that control school want to expand its exploitative functions (technical training to train workers for a wired society) and punitive controls (disciplinary rules, school uniforms, longer school years and school days, focus on basics that further habits of obedience and subservience) while criticizing therapeutic efforts (sex education, psychological counseling, self-esteem programs). But the powers that people school—the students—understand what the official agenda of school is: a concerted effort to make them into serious people. This they resist mightily though subtly. Most (but not all) find quiet ways to promote unscholastic expression, modes of anti-intellectual and sometimes anti-social rebellion, and acts of sensuality. The only way to endure the absurd seriosity of school is to find ways to have fun in the interstices of a boring and useless institution. One has to put up with the insanities of school to receive a credential and escape from the rationalized torment of the educational curriculum imposed from the authorities.

The trouble with school is that it interferes with the *popular* education of the kids (who would prefer to be "kidding around"). The curriculum of popular culture is teaching them how to be a fun person and the ways to have fun, and this conflicts with the curriculum at school designed to make them into serious people habituated to the demands of the work world specifically and the adult world generally. The authorities of school are determined that students get something out of school, whereas the students are equally determined to get out of school when they can. This has created an enormous conflict, since the serious demands of school keep expanding. By some accounts, schoolchildren have more homework than ever, and students in countries such as China and Japan spend even more time at night doing lessons. Many students feel the time crunch, since they find time for active play after school (and the great range of classes, from karate to piano to ceramics), and for many, work (often a necessity, but also to make money for the accouterments of play—a car, clothes, music, and so on). For the few who excel at school, these demands constitute no problem, but for the many who find school burdensome and even irrelevant, they are ever more reasons to hate school. Many students seek summer internships and educational programs that enhance their career chances, whereas others take classes that hasten the day they are rid of school. Apparently diminished is the idea of free time after school for daydreaming and pickup games and courtship, and summers of beach parties and backpacking in Europe and lazing around reading novels are merely social memories of a previous epoch.

As an inclusionary institution, the way most schools have dealt with a clientele of fun people is to incorporate aspects of play into their educational curriculum. There have always been ancillary activities at school that mobilized play, such as sports, plays, forensics,

field trips, clubs, elections, and so forth. Such activities are often imbued with seriosity, since they often serve a propaganda function.
But many people's best memories of school involve these playful activities. Sports have serious messages that schools want to convey,
but most students remember the thrill of agonistic play and spectacle. Indeed, sports at all levels has in many instances become a
school's core activity. Like the apocryphal coach who said he favored
academic excellence because he wanted a school the football team
could be proud of, schools have found sports to be one of their main
selling points, cash cows, reason for loyalty and enthusiasm among
students and alumni, and claim to fame. Schools public and private
may be strapped for cash to staff a physics department or equip a
language lab but find the money for sports coliseums, including
elaborate facilities for students as well as athletes. The largest edi-
fice on many campuses is the sports and recreational palace.

At the level of higher education, a whole genre of student has
emerged for whom school is a place to "hang out" for a happy time as
long as they can make it last. They define themselves as fun people
determined to resist the serious messages of school while enjoying
the opportunities for play. The much-criticized leniencies and tolera-
tions of school have allowed many students to stay around schools for
long periods of time doing marginal amounts of schoolwork but
maximal amounts of partying. The prototypical Joe Fraternity
"party animal" of campus legend is something of a role model here:
someone who thinks school is the occasion to brandish his anti-
intellectualism, to boorishly treat women as sexual playthings and
those different as things to be laughed at, someone who wears bad
manners and grotesque humor in public like a badge, and thinks the
faculty are a bunch of inferior employees he expects to pass him
through without effort. Such a social type is a residue of the changes
in school that made some define the experience as wholly play, and
the dependence of school on an entire class of students whose only
use for it was as a place to raise hell for a few years. (A popular T-shirt
around college campuses in recent years bore this message: "COL-
LEGE: The Best 5 or 6 Years of Your Life/Top Ten Things That Make
College Great—1. Two Words: Road Trip. 2. Weekends Start on
Thursdays. 3. Where Else Is 15 Hours a Week Considered a "Full
Load"? 4. Beer. 5. Parents Mistakenly Convinced You Actually Study.
6. Real World: Go to Work or Get Fired; College: Skip Class to Watch
'Beavis and Butthead.' 7. 'D' Is for Diploma. 8. Your Parents Practi-
cally Pay You to Party. 9. Sleeping 'Til Noon. 10. It's The World's Long-
est Party.") This large class of students has been crucial in redefining

the function of school toward play, and their definition of school as a play commodity has expanded its ludenic functions. Wags have long maintained that schools need to simply eliminate their irrelevant academic activities, and exist as a play institution that supports sports, parties, courtship, and the ecology of pizza parlors and bars that surrounds most campuses. In that case, the fun people will have made school into a new kind of pleasure dome that became popular simply by eliminating the play of the mind.

Colleges and universities in many Western countries, then, have made themselves over into play institutions. A walk around virtually any campus not committed to religious puritanism will reveal a complex of facilities devoted to recreation, a vast sports schedule ranging from football to field hockey, student gymnasia with every imaginable kind of fitness equipment, a student union and performance halls advertising a full and varied program of speakers, concerts, lectures, shows, and so forth, and a thriving "party culture" in fraternity and sorority houses, off-campus housing, and the entertainment culture (bars, movies, restaurants, and so on) surrounding the campus. The campus pool and dorm quadrangles in warm weather remind the onlooker of the carnival of flesh and raging hormones present on campus (with birth control easily available, often at the infirmary). The "white noise" of play becomes difficult to ignore even though serious deliberation is called for.

The play culture of higher education mitigates against seriosity. The anti-intellectualism of campus cliques is now exacerbated by the availability of fun. The "serious student" is stigmatized as not only a bookworm but also as no fun. Professors with high standards and deep subjects are avoided as "hard"; those who deal seriously with theology or poetry or history are "boring." In the competition for the critical mass of unchallenged and easily distracted students, it has become tempting to import entertainment values into courses, and indeed to teach courses about entertaining subjects. Not only do teachers use film and video more extensively, they try to teach about popular culture and mass media and celebrity—worthy subjects, but often defined by students as "hip," and thus undemanding and entertaining in themselves, defeating the critical and educative purposes of the course. Association with the play world of entertainment has now extended to academic honorifics: over the last three decades, there has been a quantum increase in the number of honorary degrees bestowed on celebrated figures from show business, sports, and other ludenic enterprises, and it is now common for commencement speakers to be drawn from the ranks of movie stars, television news celebrities, and other fields of media and popular play unrelated to serious achievement.

It is tempting to trace this to the proliferation of hip- and pop-culture-educated students, and the necessity of dealing with fun people who can't take much of anything seriously. Thus they can't take the role of "scholar" seriously at all, since that would entail participation in activities that are both demanding and alien to their experience. There is a sense in which the modal college student now is a playful alienate, someone who is an incredulous spectator of the educational process and campus life, who thinks academic seriosity a joke and understands student power as a commodity to be catered to and processed through. The educational experience expands the capacity for play, and extends the skepticism about the uses of serious learning and the cultivation of cultural sophistication. With school defined as a great place to play, it is no wonder that it serves as a vehicle for the prolongation of adolescence. The social conflict emerges as school is increasingly designed for the achievements of the driven, those few students who learn at fast rates, are highly competitive, and who figure out the "right" answers—what is officially true or sanctioned—and know how to give them. These students are playing the academic game to win, and know how to use the rules to drive to the top; the rest, who learn at slower rates, are not competitive, and are not motivated to be first and best with the school-pleasing answers, are playing the academic game to break even. Both the driven and the "laid-back" long ago in their educational experience settled on the metaphor of school as a game; once that was decided, the only remaining question was how to play the game. The driven students make up a game plan of success and glory; the playful alienates plan for the next party, spring break, and making up an easy class schedule for next semester.

The play culture has communicated many attitudes to contemporary youth, but the metaphor of life as a game is perhaps the most consequential. It connotes to young people that the game—of school, of work and career, of friendship and courtship, of parenting, of politicking—is something to be *played*. The driven are Machiavellians of the organization game: how can I use the rules to exploit the system for my academic goals? The laid-back students attempt to exploit the system to get by, and to avoid punitive sanctions and academic therapy that would make them into "good students." Throughout the course of contemporary lives, the driven will cultivate the habit of playing to win, and the laid-back will play to muddle through. But neither group will be able to take the world they either must conquer or endure as anything other than a game that must be played. They both maintain a kind of cognitive distance from what they do, as if they are observing the game under way without being taken in by its affectation of high seriousness. The world sees them as a commodity to be exploited, and the feeling appears to be mutual. For whatever reason games must be played, their skeptical and ironic approach helps them define the world as play, as amusing encounters they can take part in but still watch as incredulous spectators at a voyeuristic distance without revealing too much of themselves. The driven want to have fun winning at investing or administering or politicking, whereas everyone else just wants to think of life as, they hope, one long party. They learned all this in school.

THE STATE OF PLAY

In 1980, *Harper*'s magazine editor Lewis H. Lapham wrote that he had read Veblen and concluded that his "leisure class" had expanded into *the leisure state*.[22] What Veblen's superrich of the Gilded Age had practiced as a class privilege had become the province and habit of all those imbued with the desire for conspicuous exhibition of worth through dramatization of what one has. The democratization of leisure had brought out the fact that what the many wish to acquire is the ability to play, usually manifest in the toys of play and access to the fashionable places and times of play. In the leisure state, however, the style and trendsetters are not only the rich and famous but also the powerful. The "political class" of the nation's capital have become crucial for their leadership in the cultivation and communication of the legitimacy and importance of play. Movie stars and cafe society have been superceded in some measure by the politicians, political companions, television news celebrities and journalists, aides and administrators, lawyers and lobbyists, campaign managers and pollsters, and various socialite hangers-on and political wanna-bes in Washington and other capitals. The media search for the celebrated now shifts to, or at least adds, those Washingtonians who exemplify the narcissistic display of worth by showing their possession of, or association with, wealth, celebrity, or power. The tabloid descendants of Walter Winchell seek their prey in the corridors of power and gatherings of privilege in Washington as well as Hollywood and New York. They do so because we are interested in the privileges of play accorded the powerful.

A leisure state is led by the elite of the political state. The political class of an imperial capital rich in power and wealth assumes the leadership of social play. Such an elite is as unabashed about its enjoyment of the perquisites and payoffs of its position as Veblen's robber barons. The cozy relationship between politicians, powerful interests, the bureaucracy, the news media, and the legal establishment does not surprise or outrage many people. Such a political glitterati is a logical consequence of a leisure state, since it is by definition devoted to the enjoyment of the rewards and pleasures open to those at the top who represent the social "radiant body." The political class in such a state becomes all the more conservative and in a sense self-serving in the protection of status, and the display of privileged and conspicuous leisure becomes an important aspect of ruling. (Perhaps the favored status of the American political class in particular can be best illustrated by the astonishing triumph of a kind of hereditary principle, in which the offspring of Washington grandees and important political families exercise a right to rule based on sanguinary ties; heirs apparent are drawn from the progeny of political patricians with names such as Bush, Gore, Kennedy, Rockefeller, and so on.)

The cultural status of the political elite is safe and secure not because of its benevolence but because of its irrelevance. Historians will long ponder the present in many advanced modern countries as to why they all had vibrant economies that created unparalleled wealth and technical innovations, expansive and pluralistic popular cultures that truly offered something for everyone to play with, but at the same time, endured political systems that tended to be led by the mean-spirited, parochial, backward, and drearily partisan, and produced either endless deadlock or earnest efforts to restrict as much human freedom as possible and make life more miserable for people the powerful didn't like. In a productive sense, the political class both here and abroad has earned the contempt of economic and cultural elites.

How then do they persist? In part, by habits of obedience, but also now by habits of ridicule, for many share the view that members of the political class of such countries are inept and inconsequential. As serious political expectations have declined into hopelessness, they have been superceded by expectations of political entertainment. The only things that break up the dead rituals of electing and governing have been those events and occasions and people that exemplify the ludicrousness of the ruling elite. Most people are interested in politics only when it is fun to watch. Otherwise, it is a deadly bore to be avoided like the plague. The political world is as unreal to ordinary people as a work of comic fiction or surreal painting; it shares with art the fact that it is an aesthetic experience. People enjoy the glittering ceremonies of political theater and the show of political society that passes before them, but they also take perverse joy in the idiotic tangles and embarrassing shenanigans that surface. They like to see the state rituals that display the symbols of power; but they also love it when the facade collapses and the haughty are exposed as mere pomposities. Their favorite political narrative is "The Emperor's New Clothes."

Long ago, the philosopher David Hume argued that *opinion*—what people thought of rule and rulers—was at the base of political power. If people held an "opinion of right," they thought that one should obey, since the rulers had a legitimate right to rule. If they held an "opinion of interest," they understood it would pay them to obey, since they won by complying and lost by not. Habit teaches us the first, and power the second, but we may wonder how much strength they retain at the moment. Now these are supplemented, and perhaps superceded, by an *opinion of amusement*. People go about their lives expecting precious little that is innovative or generous from government, and little that is intelligent or brave from politics. They tolerate its self-perpetuation not because of its efficiency or rectitude but rather because it is so amusing. The popular opinion of the state and the political class may be negative as to their interests or even sense of "rightness," but it may well be positive as to their search for the risible. They are no longer citizens of the state, or active participants pursuing self-interest, but they are spectators who consume politics as a form of popular comedy.

Now, it is true that large numbers of people in the contemporary world have found other pursuits more fun. The changes in civic engagement may include for many a disengagement from the political. People involved in investing and Internet work and their own business may find their job rewarding and indeed a lot of fun. Many others find and seek cultural pursuits that make their leisure time enjoyable. Large populations range across a myriad of enterprises, but they seem to all share a contempt for, and disinterest in, the political process. One does not have to go deeply into polling to find enormous populations in many countries "turned off" by politics. Nonvoting has become the norm rather than the exception in countries such as the United States, and the number of people who watch conventions, debates, and even extraordinary events such as impeachment trials has fallen precipitously. We may opine that many of them find better things to do and follow, and that politics as usual is at last simply a bore. If boredom is the truly unbearable modern psychic condition, then the facile seriosity and rhetorical bromides of politics strike many people as not only phony but dreary. Politics cannot compete with the fun of making money or surfing the 'Net or, for that matter, surfing the California coast.

Yet for significant portions of contemporary people, politics is something they follow, even if they do not "participate" in the usual sense. These people follow politics because they find it fun. The range here is wide, from the casual people who "tune it in" when something juicy such as a scandal or war promises to be entertaining, to those political junkies who think it an enjoyable and eternally amusing pastime. They may well all be playful alienates, but like school, politics is something alien to have fun with. In a sense, for them *politics is comic therapy*. As consumers with a choice, they choose to follow politics as something so hilarious and ludicrous that it has a salutary benefit for their psychic health. They consume politics as leisure and at leisure, an inconsequential diversion as amusing as soap operas or football. (Famed journalist Henry L. Mencken liked to say that he didn't need to attend vaudeville for comic entertainment, when he could just read the *Congressional Record* for free; today we may suspect Mencken's descendants can get the same enjoyment out of watching CSPAN.)

Even many of the active participants in politics seem to bring to it a sense of play. In polities such as the United States, voting has steadily declined over the last several decades, with fewer and fewer people bothering to exercise their franchise. Larger numbers follow campaigns, and are amused by the game-show campaigning, the carnivalesque hoopla, and the extent to which candidates have to expose themselves to juvenile stunts (eating every form of ethnic food) and public humiliations (blunt questions about their private life). On the other hand, these numbers are diminished by the negative and accusatory tone of advertising and "charge and countercharge" rhetoric that prevails. But on the whole, campaigns and elections persist as light entertainment. Perhaps the bemusement of voters without expectations helps explain why they recently are attracted to candidates with celebrity standing and flashy credentials, rather than "serious" candidates with substantive achievements and plans; political bodies such as Congress and governerships are populated by play-figures such as astronauts, ex-POWs, movie actors, ex-athletes from a variety of sports, talk radio hosts, professional wrestlers, singers, and so on, all of whom seem to be there as a recognition of their popular heroics. (One recalls the line from Edward Gibbon's *Decline and Fall of the Roman Empire*: "A law was thought necessary

to discriminate the dress of comedians from that of senators. . . .")
Politics in the age of play seems to generate light but not heat; even
those engaged with it do not see it as intensely involving "deep play"
but rather as more casual, and eminently forgettable, light play.

It has been noted that political play involves a strong element of
control. The play of elites, for instance, may serve as a satisfying
show of privilege and power that reinforces the status hierarchy and
the monopoly of the instruments of rule. Rhetorical play by elite actors may serve to quell hopes and quiet fears. When some beneficial
proposal is made to alleviate some public agony, such as unavailable
health care, it is ridiculed as perverse or futile or dangerous, actually
hurting the people it is designed to help, hopeless to implement, and
involving costs and complications of unimaginable proportions. The
proposal enters public discourse as a subject of play, dismissed as so
obviously idiotic as not to warrant serious discussion. By switching
to a playful tone of derision and shared contempt, the very idea of improving public health is removed from the realm of political seriosity.
Hope is quelled among those in need, enlisting many of them among
the ranks of the alienated; those not in need are satisfied that something so hugely dumb was quashed before it could be taken seriously.
Similarly, fears of imminent danger can be quieted by denying that
the danger is there; scientific studies of global warming are dismissed as biased jeremiads, a kind of comic pseudoscience that richly
deserves our ridicule and rejection.

In an era of play politics, politicians are not only expected to make
fun of "well-intentioned but misguided" proposals, they are also expected to demonstrate that they, the leaders of government, *care*. Political identification is enhanced by gestures of familiarity: mingling,
listening, even mourning. The play of empathy establishes the polit-
ico as common and accessible. The political empathic presiding at
celebrations and rites of passage such as graduations and com-
memorations and funerals provides a ludenic experience for the
larger audience, sharing the emotion of care and reaping the benefits
of displays of caring. (With sad events such as the *Challenger* explosion and the death of Princess Diana, we are in a tricky area of experience, but it must be admitted that many people in the massive
audience for these memorials enjoyed the proceedings, and found
both catharsis and entertainment in the conduct of the televised proceedings.)

Yet the play of political control works both ways. Public play may
be a political resource, but it is also a popular expectation. Politicians
are judged by their capacity for a playful attitude, or conversely, are

condemned if they are seen as serious, boring, or moralistic. This expectation seeps its way into policy. The politics of play means that it is difficult to enforce and sustain a regime of austerity. Since a political leader is there to create the conditions for the good life, prosperity, self-indulgence, and moral tolerance are expected. Calls for frugality, moral restraint, and social reform become threats to the primary want of having fun. And, since political playfulness implies both frivolity and casual commitments, involvement in foreign entanglements, moral crusades, or improving programs become difficult, since they take enough time and effort to become irritating or boring. Foreign commitment of troops entails the difficulty of casualties, lengthy complications, and the specter of stalemate (raising the futility argument). The politics of play favors the use of symbolic gestures—a visit to a classroom, a slogan about drugs, a flurry of troop movements—rather than tangible actions that may be painful and lengthy. It has become typical of politicians that they fear most being seen as the bearer of serious tidings ("We need to do this"), and wish most of all to be seen as Dr. Feelgood. Popular desire for play constricts political options severely, since the expectation for lightness of political appearance does not allow for the strain of lifting heavy substance.

In an era of asocial entertainment and ludenic expectations, political play delimits the conduct of politics. In a sense, this is highly democratic: we are getting the government we want rather than the one we deserve. We wish it to be harmless, undemanding, and nominally caring. This means that political seriosity has to be phony: we expect governments to appear serious, but not to do serious things. Moral policy, for instance, has to be confined to Canutean gestures that urge the waves to stop; any concerted effort to act on a value—attempting to end abortions—involves the imposition of social discipline that people do not like. Indeed, the general problem of ruling a leisure state is the difficulty of imposing a regime of sacrifice, requiring austerity, compulsion, and discipline. An austere economic policy that imposes savings, delayed gratification, and reduced consumption would be wildly unpopular. Similarly, regulations to conserve energy or natural resources conflict with habits of high energy and resource use. Compulsory requirements, such as the draft, gun control, or community service are resented as unwelcome governmental interference in our lives. And attempts to impose a modicum of social discipline, ranging from fines for jaywalking to school uniforms to curfews, become a widespread irritant. All such political programs that involve abstinence or denial clash with our luxurious goals of personal self-enhancement and pleasure. Government, after all, is the agency that is supposed to further, or at least not interfere with, the pursuit of happiness.

This famous Jeffersonian phrase is now the defining criterion of governmental activity. Political austerity has been superceded by political therapeutics that shifts demand from the powerful to the populace: We, the people, demand that you not only let us play, but sustain and enhance the conditions of play. We do not want to hear warnings about "opportunity costs"; we only want to see the opportunity benefits. To deny that the pursuit of happiness is the sole purpose of life and the paramount function of governmental policy would be an act of political suicide. In some measure, all political debate in the present centers on the best way to promote and ensure the pursuit of happiness. The greatest good for the greatest number is a matter of how to create and expand the leisure state, the right of the people to exercise their ludenic rights. Since we define happiness as the opportunity to play, we have elevated play to the status of a human right. And if we think the essence of happiness is the maximization of pleasure and the minimization of pain, then the politics of play follows accordingly. Our constant if tacit message to government is: Leave us alone so that we may play.

In some measure, the political triumph of the play principle may well be seen as the democratization of the optimistic Enlightenment faith in popular rights. It can also be seen as a descendant of the Utopian socialist and Marxian vision of a world freed of unnecessary labor. We now focus less on the justice of the division of labor and more on the prerogatives of the division of leisure. The popular right to play becomes enshrined as something that cannot be taken away. If we not only want but also *need* to play, then political inhibition of the therapeutic reward of play becomes an explosive delimitation of popular benefits, thought to have been won as a political right. Political scientists have long recognized that in large modern societies, the government budget is always too small (and paradoxically, always too large). Most such governments maintain elaborate benefit structures: France provides "culture vouchers" for the unemployed to gain access to museums, concerts, lectures, and the like; Norway sends citizens with mental problems off to the Canary Islands for six weeks; the Germans send ill people to spas; and all maintain elaborate and expensive medical, retirement, and public health benefits, which frees up much private wealth to be utilized in retirement or leisure time for healthy people to play. Environmental protection stems not only from the demand for clean air and water and so on, but also from the popular desire for a "green" environment that includes parks, trails, forests, lakes, and so forth for leisure activities. In this new political dispensation, the function of government is to provide ludenic benefits, as if there is a new corollary to the Bill of Rights: *The right of the people to play shall not be infringed upon.*

NOTES

1. Samuel P. Hays, "Theoretical Implications of Recent Work in the History of American Society and Politics," *History and Theory* 26, no. 1 (1987): pp. 15–31.

2. Robert D. Putnam, "Bowling Alone: America's Declining Social Capital," *Current* 373 (June 1995): pp. 3–9.

3. Jules Henry, *Culture Against Man* (New York: Random House, 1963), p. 13.

4. Juliet B. Schor, *The Overworked American: The Unexpected Decline of Leisure* (New York: Basic Books, 1991).

5. Rifkin, Jeremy, *The End of Work* (New York: Putnam, 1996); Ralf Dahrendorf, "The End of the 'Labor Society'," *World Press Review* (March 1983): pp. 27–29; Robert Frank and Phillip Cook, *The Winner-Take All Society* (New York: The Free Press, 1995).

6. Richard Klein, *Cigarettes Are Sublime* (Durham: Duke University Press, 1995); James Atlas, "The Fall of Fun," *The New Yorker* (November 18, 1996): 61–71.

7. Neil Postman, *Teaching as a Conserving Activity* (New York: Dell, 1979), p. 50.

8. Arnold Rose, "Popular Logic in the Study of Covert Culture," in *Theory and Method in the Social Sciences* (Minneapolis: University of Minnesota Press, 1954), p. 323.

9. Neil Postman, *Amusing Ourselves to Death* (New York: Viking Penguin, 1986), p. 87.

10. Michael J. Wolf, *The Entertainment Economy* (New York: Times Books, 1999).

11. Jane Kuentz, et al., *Inside the Mouse: Work and Play at Disney World* (Durham: Duke University Press, 1997); Henry A. Giroux, *The Mouse That Roared: Disney and the End of Innocence* (Blue Ridge Summit, PA: Rowman & Littlefield, 1999).

12. Hugh D. Duncan, *Communication and Social Order* (New York: The Bedminster Press, 1962), pp. 347–369.

13. Thomas Frank, *The Conquest of Cool* (Chicago: University of Chicago Press, 1997).

14. Robert Goodman, *The Luck Business* (New York: The Free Press, 1995).

15. Suzanne Woolley, "The Big Thrill," *Money*, April 1999, p. 29.

16. W. Terrence Gordon, *Marshall McLuhan: Escape into Understanding* (New York: Basic Books, 1997).

17. James W. Carey, "A Cultural Approach to Communication," *Communication,* 2d ed. (1975): pp. 6, 8.

18. Robert Jewett and John Shelton Lawrence, *The American Monomyth,* 2 ed. (New York: University Press of America, 1988), pp. 159–161.

19. Victor Turner, ed., Introduction to *Celebration: Studies in Festivity and Ritual* (Washington: Smithsonian Institution Press, 1982), pp. 11, 16; Harold Garfinkel, "Conditions of a Successful Degradation Ceremony," in *Drama in Life,* ed. James E. Combs and Michael W. Mansfield (New York: Hastings House, 1976), pp. 315–321.

20. Neal Gabler, *Winchell: Gossip, Power, and the Culture of Celebrity* (New York: Knopf, 1994).

21. Theodore Roszak, *The Making of a Counter Culture* (Garden City, NY: Doubleday Anchor, 1969).

22. Lewis H. Lapham, *Fortune's Child* (Garden City, NY: Doubleday, 1980), pp. 320–322.

CHAPTER 3

The Futuristics of Play: The Prospect for the Ludenic Condition

Alas, the right of the people to play may well be infringed upon. Even though the historical dynamic has expanded the opportunity to play, and the practice of play has become ingrained in our lives as a modern habit and asserted right, there is no temporal guarantee like a play insurance policy that assures us a future of more and better play. At the cusp of a new century, it is always tempting to engage in social forecasting that assuredly predicts the future. More parsimoniously, we will say only that we are in a *liminal* age, on the threshold of several possible historical outcomes for both the near and far future. Perhaps the way to proceed here is to reflect on the possible social meanings of the rise of the play world, then speculate on the potential for a large-scale reaction against play, and finally, ponder the features of a future world at play. We will then conclude with some valedictory and salutatory thoughts about the nature of play.

PONDERING THE DYNAMIC OF PLAY

Let us assume that our thesis is correct that the social activity of play has been an expansive and innovative force in contemporary life. If that is the case, perhaps we should ponder briefly what this dynamic force means. Why, in the late twentieth century, did large numbers of people in modern and not-so-modern countries manage to find the time and energy to engage in various forms of play? Why

did a cultural activity long thought to be ancillary or even illegitimate acquire such importance in so many people's lives? Why play
now? Several competing explanations, not necessarily mutually exclusive, may be pondered. But these are post hoc hypotheses; we are
in the usual position of explaining a cultural phenomenon that is already happening. By the time we notice something such as the dy-
namo of play, it has already wrought its impact. But let us try.

Response to Chaotic Change

Liminal periods are characterized by rapid innovation and con-
fusing orientation. In a time of the shock of the new, newness creates
the conditions for disorientation. When the world seems chaotic, the
way to create, or re-create, meaning is to revert to play. This can involve reversion to and rediscovery of old arrangements and beliefs or
the embrace of new things. In the former instance, the emergence of
political conservatism and fundamentalist religion is likely play
with the sure and venerable. In a world dominated by mindless technique and the whirl of immediacy, people hope to find identity and
community in political or religious absolutism. The wandering and
searching "protean self" can find respite and refuge in the strictures
and rituals of ideology and theology. In the warmth of political or religious gatherings, one can feel fellowship and certainty in the symbolic assertion of right. Such gatherings are not so much
communities of value or interest as they are ludenic, since they serve
to revitalize the world with magical powers to transform. Play occurs
in an enchanting time and space, and such ceremonies, it is hoped,
re-enchant life with old but newly vital symbols that give the com-
municants sanctified powers. Among such groupings, there are recurrent calls for this new political or religious elect to act on these
renewed powers, but for many the play of identification with moral
surety and superiority is enough. The mode of expression in such social groups favors dramatic self- and alter-casting in rhetorical jeremiads but little direct action. The assertions of seriosity in such
groups is leavened by their smug amusement at the folly of their enemies and their vivid imagination of the wickedness of the fallen
world. Puritan fervor or partisan fanaticism is mitigated by a comic
view of the world outside the magic circle, with the fear of the dark
designs of their enemies eased by knowledge of their foes' foolhardy
self-destruction. We may expect that such affiliations will persist
into the tumult of the near future, but we may also wonder if such
ideological or theological play will be enough to satisfy true believ-
ers. If enchanting play is sufficient, we will have less of a warring

crusade and more of a defensive stance, self-dramatization rather than the sociodrama of a movement. The failure of the larger society to embrace political agendas or moral strictures that would introduce massive restrictions on freedom and fun inspires heavy expressions of outrage and frustration at the immorality and neglect of the many, but such rhetoric gives more weight to the sense of moral superiority among the elect than it spreads shame among the damned.

The fallen many respond to chaotic change by adherence to their habits of secular coping and consumption. In the early twenty-first century, we may expect the great mass of people in the prosperous world to seek a modicum of that prosperity but also find moments of fulfillment in the enchantment of play. The work world will likely continue to change so much that older people will barely recognize it, with large populations made redundant by the rapidity and complexity of economic innovation. In that case, it will be difficult for them to find meaning in an economy that uses them and passes them by; it will be much more appealing to find meaning in play. For most people, this will entail involvement in popular culture. If they have little interest in the play of rhetorical identifications with religion or politics, and cannot find fulfillment in a work world that views them as utterly expendable, then playful cultural activity will become the future mode of fun, and not incidentally, also the source of social learning about the meaning of life. The "postmodern" popular culture now emerging—theme parks, gambling spas, fun towns, concerts and races, sports, the vast expanse of movies and TV and music—all will be the significant center of many people's lives. In a sense, attention to popular culture satisfies both conserving and liberating wants. Following sports, for instance, allows the fan to engage in a timeless and rule-governed universe more predictable and delightful than the work world or political world, and certainly less harmful or hateful. But sports also permits the emergence of innovation, surprise, rhythm and flow, the experience of community victory and defeat, the recognition of talent drawn from all segments of society, the celebration of the spirit of play.

This leads us to a distinction that may be useful in understanding future play. We may distinguish between *anarchic* play, *ritual* play, and *creative* play. Anarchic play emerges in incipient or ambiguous situations in which experimenting or probing leads to playful activity. Early childhood is the obvious example, in which young children learn through playing, fiddling with things, making up fantasies such as imaginary friends, daydreaming and playacting, and so on. The early stages of sexual relations—girl meets boy, for instance—can be charged with anarchic play, fumbling and embarrassing trial and error as to the quality and endurance of the relationship. But play develops into habits, or play with certain rules. Children learn how to play games: a pickup game with a stick and ball evolves into baseball. The passionate play of new lovers becomes routinized into "going together" or eventually marital bliss. Play becomes predictable and threatens to become less than playful, unless innovation or revitalization restores the vivacity and thus enchanted status of play.

For twenty-first century populations, ritual play will likely be the norm. For those enclaved groups who relish rhetorical self-definition as superior or at least different, ritual play will likely consist of endless rounds of group gatherings that provide consensual validation of their lofty position in the status hierarchy and moral universe. Popular culture will provide the setting and rules for the many to attend and understand play. If gambling continues to proliferate, then casino facilities will provide the attractive setting and gaming rules within which people can bet. In theory, gambling could be available virtually everywhere, including the gambling of day trading on stocks, bonds, and commodities around the clock and around the world through "e-trade" sites, as well as Internet gambling that accesses gaming sites where one can bet on virtually anything. (Will the old-time numbers racket and bookie joint make a comeback on the Net?) In all cases, ritualized popular culture is stylized: anarchic improvisation is eliminated in the ritual format of the theme park and ocean cruise and sports playoff. Such formats are designed experiences providing fun. But they run the danger of becoming so formalized that they become a bore. (This problem is arising in the astonishing theme park glut around Orlando, Florida: with seven stupendous parks—Disney's Kingdoms, Sea World, Universal Studios, and so on—now open, and more on the way, competition for the dollars of jaded tourists may become savage, especially if people find other vacation choices more appealing and affordable, and, most terrifying to corporate bottom-liners, if kids begin to find theme parks a big bore.)

Creative play manages to retain the vitality and experimentation of anarchic fooling around within the context of social expectations and formats that evolve into rituals. It has oft been noted that the most exciting and fruitful period of a new technology is during the incipient period when people are still playing around with it and before it settles into predictable routines and familiar formulas. The early years of the movies and television have been much heralded as creative play, when the people involved in making early movies (D. W. Griffith, Chaplin) and live television (Ernie Kovacs, *Your Show of Shows*) had enough freedom and ignorance to try new things without undue ritual constraints. Later these mediums, like all others, became less playful and therefore less creative, but they did become familiar and predictable in their media rituals—the Western, the TV sitcom, and so on.

Today, and for the near future, the mediational site of creative play is and will be the Internet. In such playful periods, enthusiasts for the new medium find enchanted community and redemptive powers in the new technology of communications. In this way it resembles religious or political movements in their dynamic phase, when the playful qualities are still obvious before they are married to prosaic utility and eventually institutional necessity. Now the "children of the Net," it is opined, have found an enchanting faith in the metaphysical knowledge gleaned on the Internet. Like those affiliated with the New Right, the "Gen Xers" and "Gen Yers" must live in a world seemingly without coherence. Surfing the Net and conquering cyberspace becomes both a personal and affiliative drama, one that differentiates and delivers them from previous mundane existence. The new technology puts the Net-Gen in touch with information, which is the global touchstone of the never-sleeping Internet eye, the light of which illuminates our lives with universal if diffuse knowledge, and makes the computer wired to the world an "emblem of salvation." The universal light never goes out, warming us with the sun of Revelation: "And there shall be no night there; and they shall need no candle, nor light of the sun." The mythology of the Net is a new gnosticism, with its central image of a universal mind and disembodied souls embarking on a spiritual quest for higher truth. Our participation in the transcendent world of the Net makes us "discarnate" beings, whose existence is melded into the noetic Mind.[1]

The Internet, then, is the latest medium that is the site of play. Telegraphers used to fill time between serious messages with playful byplay, exchanging short messages up and down the line. Now anyone can do this with e-mail, chat rooms, and so forth. But will this new kind of play make the Net-Geners different? They now grow up with this astounding access to the world's knowledge and variety, including the unsavory and lurid. Whereas the baby boomers grew up with the one-to-many technological knowledge of television, the Net-scopers are immersed in a digital universe in which they seek knowledge to use. Television play involved passive watching and learning, like Tertullian's heavenly observers of hell; Net play involves actively navigating in search of likeable information or the discarnate company of the like-minded. Net-Geners become accustomed to assembling knowledge, putting it together as they find it in their voyages. They tend to communicate many-to-many, anchoring here and there at playsites that are fun. Some observers find them acutely interconnected and innovative, independent and curious, people for whom school is a crushing bore but who are willing to learn on their own through Netplay.[2] Others have a darker view of the discarnate world of Netdwellers: that they are creating a world of social isolates afraid of human contact, whose fun is anomic and often perverse, and who exist in a netherworld of disaffection and impersonal contact with other alienates who meet only in the cyberspace of lost and wandering souls.

In any case, we may expect that the kids will continue "playing the future." They are used to discontinuity and nonlinear thinking, and see chaos as the normal condition of life, using the media at their disposal to learn how to navigate an identity voyage. This may be a discarnate identity that mitigates against physical or social contacts, but it is play learning about their future life in Netspace. If the television generation was formed by the convergent selectivity of the medium, the Net generation is being formed by the divergent selectivity they learn from their mediated experience. Television imposed a vision of life; the Internet poses a challenge to find a unique vision of life. Those visions may be quite varied and some even insane, but they may constitute the new animating impetus for Gen Xers and Yers to play their way into identity. In that sense, the learning of the Internet may be therapeutic play for the "children of chaos" coping with a world that is at once turbulent and stagnant. The activity of Net play gives them hope for a vital and animating sense of meaning, to seek and find in the ether of cyberspace a new land of enchantment.[3]

Play Is a Historical Interlude

This is the view that play becomes prominent in ludenic periods of uncertainty and change, on the way to the establishment of a new seriosity. Periods of civilization formation and reformation, creativity and innovation, and rapid and unsettling change give new vigor and meaning to playful activities. It has oft been noted that the times and places of great aesthetic receptivity—Periclean Athens, Elizabethan England, Renaissance Italy, Berlin in the Weimar period, among others—are characterized by great upheaval and change. The inter-lude provides the conditions for the emergence of an exciting and experimental spirit. Here play is crucial to the sudden bursts of creativity that unexpectedly appear, wherein the combination of crisis and hope leads people to transcend habitual modes of expression for new and imaginative forms.[4]

It may be a stretch to think of contemporary America as such a time and place. But interludes of play may also be witnessed in periods of cultural waxing and waning. In his famous work *The Autumn of the Middle Ages*, historian Johan Huizinga recounted the slow but sure eclipse of the cultural forms of the medieval period and the movement toward the new and vibrant spirit of the Renaissance and the incipient glimmerings of modernity. The changes in popular symbols and expression of such a time suggest the appearance of *temporal interplay*, a period in which ludenic activity—popular poetry and song, codes of personal conduct and etiquette, folkways of courtship and romance, and so on—subtly changes. The medieval spirit was becoming decadent and even preoccupied with death, whereas new and vibrant forms of expression brought playfulness and hopefulness into the world.[5] The emphasis here is that play-forms augur the passage from one form of life to another.

But from what to what in the present? Does the advent of new and often bizarre forms of play augur the transition from one way of living to another? The assumption appears to be that as one form of social seriosity breaks down, a liminal period of play leads to the establishment of a new form of seriosity. Play is here less of a reflexive response to change and more of the social activity that expresses and directs change. That new seriosity can be quite reactive: the Nazi revolution of the 1930s in Germany was in part a reaction against the wild and liberative play of Weimar, which was repressed and revenged by the highly punitive regime of Nazism. The appearance of play that can be labeled "decadent" or "immoral" calls for the imposition of an even more severe seriosity. Or, if one is drawn to the "decline and fall" model of history, the play of the present can be seen as a symptom of imperial decadence, reminiscent of Rome in the third century C.E. or France in the late eighteenth century. The wretched excess of the consumptive play of the superrich, or the nihilistic play of youth subcultures such as rave, techno, or Goth, constitute evidence of the decadence of the present, promising a fall from ascendancy and power because of excessive or morally damaging devotion to playing. Here the interlude of play is a descent into either effete or barbaric activities unworthy of a mighty and rich empire, and presages the eclipse of those qualities that had made for greatness. Those consumed by play are eventually overwhelmed and

even overrun by those motivated and emboldened by a morally up-
right or politically ambitious seriosity. The fear is that important
segments of society, notably elites of the large cities and educated
youth, become unwilling to defend serious myths and interests at
the core of the civilization.

The turn of the millennium has made some even speculate that
popular play in the present augurs the advent of a period of neofeu-
dalism. The great economist Schumpeter predicted "the march into
Socialism"; now we foresee a "march into Feudalism." It has been observed that the post–Cold War period and *Pax* Americana resembles
the breakup of the Roman world and the descent of Europe into the
Dark Ages. Corporations pay fealty to other corporations abroad,
without the bother anymore of an imperial allegiance or defense;
they pay tribute to warlords in barbarian lands in order to do business; lords and barons live in towers and castles guarded from the
marauding vassals and serfs; and monastic orders in universities
and Silicon Valley barbicans create the new scholastic method and il-
luminate the scrolls that constitute wisdom. The popular art of our
age playfully celebrates our fantasies about a neomedieval
age—from *Dungeons and Dragons* and *Doom* cyberspace games to
movie space operas (notably the *Star Wars* cycle) to Goth dress and
dance to occult philosophy to herbal medicine to *Camelot* fantasies
about the return of the good king. Much popular play treats the inse-
curity and confusion by depiction of catastrophe—atomic, social, ecological, migratory, chiliastic—giving impetus to religious and
survivalist cults who anticipate an imminent end to civilization and
life along with more general fears about the barbarians at the gate or
the secluded isolation of elites out of touch and out of control. Nettled
by the worry that all paranoid fantasies come true, the popular
imagination plays with a future that builds on or destroys the ruins
of the old civilization.[6]

Play Is a Passing Fancy

This is a dismissive explanation, generally stated in terms of ob-
sessive play as a fad of the culture of frivolity that emerged from the
popular cultural storm of the late twentieth century. The cult of play
emerged from the great increase in mass wealth, permissive parenting and schooling, and the bombardment of messages from popular
fare, advertising, and celebrity worship. But the argument here is
that play eventually is an unsatisifying bore, and that young people
jaded by excessive consumption, pleasure, and self-indulgence will
turn to more edifying pursuits, such as the serious quest for knowl-

edge, spirituality, and responsible citizenship. Contemporary play is not so much a response to change or a quest in a historical interlude as it is a bad habit that can and should be broken. Much political and ideological rhetoric exhorts people to eschew fun and embrace virtue. The "virtue industry" believes that it is on the side of the angels and that appeals to our "moral sense" will aright our strayed moral gyroscopes toward the virtuous life. Temporarily, people were lured by the false promise of indulgent play, but good sense will prevail over the mad lust for fun and frolic. This is a basic tenet of neoconservatism and evangelism, but shared by many others of different persuasions who find unauthorized play to be a social threat.

The merit of this view is that the level and extent of access to play expanded exponentially in the last half of the twentieth century, so it can be argued that the circumstances of the play explosion were almost unique. Never before had so many people had so much money, ability to travel, good health and energy, and freedom before. Given that, they were drawn to play as never before. But the god of play turned out to be a false god, reaching the Dionysian excesses of the 1960s and 1970s before beginning the return to normal seriosity. The difficulty is that evidence is pretty scant that this return to sane normalcy and moral decorum has retaken the world from the idols of play. Play has become a habit and expectation, and calls for the restoration of modesty, sobriety, courtesy, gentility, and other serious personal virtues become difficult to implement. (If there is to be a "return to modesty," someone had better alert the fashion industry and the supermodels parading shamelessly down catwalks.)

It may be true that play is a passing fancy, but not as a historical thesis; rather playtime may for many be a passing fancy of an increasingly extended period in their lives of willful immaturity, in which they continue to enjoy play as a pleasure of delayed childhood, adolescence, and a "swinging single" lifestyle. A major locus of play that the agents of seriosity find reprehensible is among groups who maintain a playful life rather than accept "mature" roles and responsibilities. For many people, immaturity is more fun. Moviegoing has become an infantile experience in which people talk and disrupt the show, and laugh at both seriously shocking or tenderly sensual scenes, combining childish cuteness and juvenile wise-guy derision of adult seriosity. For those who find maturity threatening, or in adulthood decide to seek out their "inner child," doing childish things becomes an expression of their eternal, or at least extended, youthfulness. Middle-aged people who continue to live like students—slovenly apartments, all-night parties, sleeping around,

hanging out, casually taking and quitting jobs—have delayed adolescence beyond youth but retain the youthful lifestyle that refuses
the trappings of maturity even as one physically ages. If we think of
youth as a fun time and adulthood as a dreary time, then the temptation to be like Peter Pan, to remain forever young by having fun, becomes irresistible, given the alternatives. In the 1950s, one of the
century's great serious men, George F. Kennan, saw Southern California's culture of easy money and morals as one promoting endless
"childhood without the promise of maturity," creating a people who
were unready for any eventual "day of reckoning and hardship."[7]
Now the "California dreaming" ideal is worldwide, since maturity
seems more of a threat than a promise, and days of reckoning can be
delayed forever. California has become a worldwide symbol of carefree play in a hedonic lotusland, an endless summer of eternal youth
and beauty and fun. Perhaps the truly enduring legacy of Ronald
Reagan is to teach us that the purpose of prosperity is to become a
California person, forever youthful and handsome and relaxed and
tanned, turning all discourse into the form of a jest and democracy
into a fun-house distortion of the ideal. Political seriosity becomes a
passing fancy that can safely be dismissed by that staple of youthful
snideness, the wisecrack, which confidently reasserts the delusion-
ary state of relaxed lightness with no conscious fear of a day of reckoning and hardship.

Indeed, the attitude and expression of youthful insolence and de-
risiveness toward the serious world pervades the popular culture.
We now celebrate, in a variety of venues such as radio talk shows,
punditic debate shows, late-night television, and situation comedies,
the gathering of groups of young or youngish people who represent
states of immaturity. Their conceit is to bash maturity in the form of
seriosity and mature acts such as changing your mind or admitting
failure. For instance, talk radio shows often consist of groups of
males who like to denigrate and humiliate women, talk about subjects frivolous or serious with loutish humor or insults, and in general behave like a bunch of bratty kids horsing around. Political
punditic shows are a slight cut above this, but usually age-regress to
a shouting and baiting match. And so on. It is tempting to speculate
that in a postimperial age, with the male population aging, less fertile, and required to respect female equality, this play with immaturity is a reaction to perceived threat.[8] Regression into juvenile play
groups we either join or watch becomes a fad that helps people cope
with social change. Once they get used to change, they will become
responsible adults and no longer need outlets for immature expres-

sion. California dreaming and macho woman bashing will become dated as an embarrassingly childish artifact of an age of transition to a more mature culture.

This "getting used to" explanation, if valid, would mean that play is a passing fancy in people's lives. Perhaps in a larger sense what is happening is that many people are getting bored with play! The wide world of play itself becomes a passing fancy insufficient to satisfy our need for meaning and purpose. Adults acting like children, for instance, activates our repulsion of what Huizinga once called "Puerilism," or "that blend of adolescence and barbarity" that fuels "the insatiable thirst for trivial recreation and crude sensationalism." This sort of unsatisfying activity is in fact "false play" because "puerilism is to be distinguished from playfulness." Adults acting like children (Huizinga has the Nazis in mind) turns the province of children into an adult refusal to become mature, making the role of merry prankster into a social norm and narcissistic self-indulgence into the quintessence of fun. But civilized playfulness eventually is reasserting itself, and we may expect the passing fancy of the puerile culture to wane as the lure of overstimulation and irresponsibility becomes a bore at last.[9]

Play Augurs the Emergence of a New Civilization

We will return to this thesis at the conclusion of the book. Suffice it to say here that whatever the merits of the explanations above, they all see the contemporary emergence of the play culture as temporary. In the first explanation, the world is changing and play becomes the locus of new learning; in the second, the world is in an interlude, and play becomes either a momentary respite or reorientation toward the imminence of innovation; in the third, the world is intolerable, so the impulse is to both reject and attack it by adopting the viewpoint and behavior of immaturity. Now, these explanations are neither exhaustive nor mutually exclusive, but they do seem to share the idea that the growth of the play culture occurs in a *post-intellectual society*. Such a society by definition has less use for traditional forms and habits of intellect that have characterized the modern world. The changes from an intellectual to postintellectual world include the decline of critical thinking, knowledge displaced by "information," literary and cultural illiteracy, reality experienced through media, popular rather than high culture, loss of privacy, and so on.[10] To the postintellectual thesis we may add two assertions: *the post-intellectual world is moving us from seriosity to play, and we are not witnessing something temporary but rather something that consti-*

tutes a major innovation that has the potential to transform the way we live. The above explanations do not sufficiently see the advent of play as part of a larger historical process that is fundamentally changing the world, for good or ill. These views fail to see play as a primal condition and expectation of the world to come. Developmental analysis posits that if certain patterns continue, the potential for *the ludenation of the world* is a possible, but not necessary, outcome of temporal processes. There may be intervening factors, or countermovements, that inhibit the spread and growth of play as a social habit. Let us now look at those forces that might inhibit the growth of the pattern of social play in the future.

AGAINST PLAY: THE DANGERS OF TOO MUCH FUN

One of the great contributions of the twentieth century to social forecasting has been *the dystopian imagination*. Writers such as Kafka, Orwell, Huxley, and various science fiction writers have both enriched and horrified us with their negative images of what we were becoming. Nonfiction writers have complemented these imaginary dystopias with analysis that agreed that the poets are indeed right: we will not become freer, richer, happier, or to the point here, have a lot more fun. Rather we will suffer all sorts of social and environmental maladies that will take away hope for a great increase in the quality and lightheartedness of our lives. Dystopian visions range from imaginings of chaos to control. In the former case, the world of tomorrow is seen as devolving into a maelstrom of unmanageable conditions—environmental degradation, overpopulation, a reversion to barbarism, the decline and fall of empires and the rise of marauding vandals and bandits, the collapse of civilization. These horrors are not just the mad visions of apocalyptic prophets. Noted economist Robert L. Heilbroner famously concluded of the "human prospect": "If then, by the question 'Is there hope for man?' we ask whether it is possible to meet the challenges of the future without the payment of a fearful price, the answer must be: No, there is no such hope." The future is bleak except for those places that institute Draconian controls, blending "a 'religious' orientation with a 'military' discipline."[11] Such monastic controls do indeed conjure up the religious orders of the Dark Ages after the fall of Rome, with monks in Ireland and elsewhere surviving the chaos outside by becoming self-sufficient and clinging to their faith. In any case, the thrust of the dystopian visions of both chaos and control posit *a future that is no fun.*

Of special interest to us here are those projective imaginings wherein control in the future is maintained through the manipulation of play. Huxley's *Brave New World*, published in 1932, outlined how administered play could increase the efficiency of benevolent totalitarianism. "The problem of happiness," he later remarked of his vision, will be "the problem of making people love their servitude." Happiness could be engineered by convincing people that their lives were enriched by access to sexual variety, drugs that made them content, gentle propaganda that reduced life to slogans, and the "infinite appetite for distractions."[12] This future puerilism would reduce all of us to a regimen of false play through the manipulation of pleasure and the elimination of critical seriosity. But even though the games and diversions and free love all might seem pleasurable, in an odd sense there is no real fun in the sense of spontaneous and freely expressed joy. The thrills allowed are all engineered to direct behavior toward socially desirable conformity and contentment, but only a few suspect that the play provided is phony and that they are being conned into thinking that their distractions are good fun. Real play would involve a choice, and real playfulness a carefree spirit. In Huxley's future, play is a behaviorally induced habit as routine and unreflexive as brushing your teeth. In this kind of future, the administration of play becomes the ultimate form of human control. Postintellectualism is institutionalized as a totally mindless and conditioned society controlled through the illusion of fun.

In this dystopian vision, then, play has its uses. In the near future, perhaps the greater threat to the growth of the play culture are those people who have no use for play. For play always seems to stimulate antiplay; perhaps the world is divided into the party of play ("Let's have fun") and the party of antiplay ("Fun is bad and must be stopped"). The party of antiplay may have a variety of motives—religious or moral conviction, the belief that society requires an occasional "return of repression," a political or economic agenda, or even simple jealousy of those people who are having fun while we can't—but the impulse is *to restore to its proper place in society the hegemony of seriosity.* In the foreseeable future, for the party of antiplay to triumph, serious conditions would have to emerge that would give impetus to a campaign against play. Since play has become so ingrained as a habit and expectation, social authorities would have to have good reasons to inhibit the implied right and freedom to play. Fun would have to acquire a stigma, as something that is bad for us and therefore must be curtailed or banned. But this development, or more precisely counter-movement, will require certain conditions:

economic scarcity, cultural mobilization, and political reaction. Since it would take considerable power to disestablish play, it likely would take a concert of all three of these conditions to create a less playful and more serious future.

Economic Scarcity

The growth of play in the twentieth century occurred in an economic environment of expanding prosperity. Even with the intervention of wars and depressions, and an unequal distribution of wealth, the spread of affluence made play available to ever greater numbers of people. Former communist countries and Third World areas are rapidly and desperately trying to create the conditions for abundance by holding out the hope to their populations that concerted effort now will eventually bring the pleasures of play enjoyed by the leisure classes of the West into their lives as well. But despite the best efforts of central bankers and economists, there is no guarantee that the upward march of prosperity will continue. A sustained downturn of the world economy could change the dynamic of play in the future.

The familiar cycle posited by classical economists—a vigorous initial phase of work, savings, investment, and ambition, followed by an abundant but increasingly decadent phase of consumption, debt, and leisure, inevitably resulting in loss of will and economic decline—could be repeated. The collapse of Rome, the feudal system, and capitalism in 1929 resulted in long periods of political chaos and economic ruin. If the early twenty-first century experiences such a decline, all the oracular pronouncements of the high priests of central banks, the brave talk of a new economy, and confident predictions of an ever-higher stock market by the gurus of Wall Street will begin to sound tinny. Great economic idols who previously were objects of media admiration will be seen as charlatans, the cheerleaders of financial publications and channels will begin to sound laughable, and the great burst bubble of the bull market's glamour stocks (such as the Internet companies) will be compared to tulip mania in seventeenth-century Holland.

Most of all, in such a reduced and pinched economic atmosphere, the celebrated play of the famous, the conspicuous consumption of the rich, and the encouragement of the winner-take-all kleptomania of the acquisitive by the political class will become a subject of social criticism. Since the rest of us will be required to practice austerity, gaudy displays of "excessive" wealth, a frivolous attitude that connotes uncaring contempt for the common struggle to make do, and political hobnobbing with the idle rich will arouse democratic ire. We may expect that the popular arts will celebrate the virtues of those forced into austerity and penury, and denigrate the sins of those whose vanity and greed brought about the mass plight they refuse to share. Economic metaphysics will point out the cardinal and venal sins of the ruling class, including a puritanical condemnation of the frivolous attitude and indulgent play that characterizes our worthless elites. Ways will be found for the rich and famous and mighty to atone, including perhaps Savonarolan bonfires that purge the vain of the glittering things that possess them. (Can we imagine such shameful objects as stretch limos committed to the flame as part of the purification rite?)

In a future period of economic scarcity, not only could the play of the possessing classes be redefined as evil, but the definition of economic virtue could be renewed, extolling those Weberian characteristics of early capitalism—frugality, sobriety, productivity, caution, in general a no-nonsense approach to one's vocation and life that excludes folly such as play. Play might be regarded as the sin against the economic Holy Ghost, since it is damned as idleness, a "waste of time," useless activity, and destructive of seriosity. Play could be further suspect since it was the social culprit that robbed us of the now absent plenty, so we must redouble our serious efforts and vigilance against the lure of folly. Such a new emphasis on "life as real, life as earnest" will enjoy the support of social authorities desperate to restore some measure of abundance. Future Ministries of Plenty will then say much about "back to basics," the dignity of labor, the seriousness of the situation requiring sacrifice and common effort of all, and will perhaps even banish the "game" metaphor from economic thought as a concept altogether too frivolous. All of this would have the hoped-for effect of restoring the moral economy, which balances abundance with serious respectability, progress with wise use of wealth, and morally sanctioned play that complements rather than supplants the serious life.

Cultural Mobilization

The growth of the play culture may be challenged and curtailed by the social force of a moral crusade. This might well accompany the reinstitution of the moral economy, but in any case it would involve the mobilization of those who see play as a threat to cultural morality. Such a countermovement would aim for the remoralization of society, including all the forms of play. Such a *Kulturkampf* would attempt to involve institutions such as school in moral regimentation, and the state in an agenda of moral regulation. The explosion of the play culture, as well as other major social innovations, creates a climate for *moral panic*, wherein anxiety over a potentially threatening event or innovation translates into fearful action focused on defeating or purging the threat.[13] It is now common for moral authorities to perceive threats from popular culture and popular behavior. Eminent moralists of the Right ritually condemn the depiction of sex, violence, and coarse language in popular entertainments, and moralists of the Left condemn sexual exploitation and rapine in college-age partying and coupling. That popular cultural depravity and young male culpability may well be bogeymen is quite possible. But hitherto most such condemnations have been confined to rhetorical and symbolic gestures. Given the right conjunction of events and innovations, those with cultural power could move to shut down people's fun. The old Puritan impulse to "clean up" the culture could aim at those popular products that are blamed for teenage pregnancies, school and church shootings, and public cursing (with the astounding argument that guns don't kill people, but movies do). And the neo-Puritan impulse to control and punish sexual behavior and funning and frolicking could expand on college campuses by the imposition of pristine rules about drinking, dating, and gatherings. With both the Right and Left, we could well consider the suspicion that behind this is a deeper fear at work, the fear of people having altogether too much fun. They share, for instance, a fear of "sexual anarchy," heightened by the expanse of sexual freedom and the persistence of human messiness in gender relations. In an effort to impose order on the feared triumph of libertine sensuality, Right and Left could unite in a moral crusade to crush the infamy of fun. Ideological differences could be overcome in their shared determination to restore the hegemony of seriosity.

Indeed, a cultural agenda of "remoralization" has even led some ideologues to express admiration for the social arrangements of the Victorian age. Recent tomes have extolled the virtues of the English poor laws, orphanages, and workhouses, familial and sexual respectability (in the American nineteenth century, a respectable woman was expected to be devoid of passion and to express "becoming abhorrence" to sexual overtures, even from her husband), modesty, shame, even good posture. Somehow contemporary intellectuals, appalled by the lighthearted spirit and freewheeling culture of the late twentieth century, and fearing descent into an abyss of people preoccupied with having fun and pursuing pleasure, have decided that the Victorians were the superior culture, apparently because they were very serious. The moral virtues we are alleged to have lost the Victorians are thought to have had in abundance: social discipline, intense family loyalties, moral certitude, self-reliance, and cleanliness. Shameful approbation and punishment was directed at stigmatized people associated with unproductive idleness and illegitimate and immoral play: prostitutes and unwed mothers, the "undeserving" poor, the drunks who hung around pubs and gin mills, bohemians and homosexuals, orphans and beggars and chimney sweeps and mudlarks, indeed all those whose failed character led them to waste time and reject respectability. The fantasy then as now is that there was and is a vast underworld (or "underclass") of parasitical and cunning people engaged in figuring out how to live well by not working, bilking the system, and spending their idle days at play. This Victorian projection of armies of the morally blighted enjoying themselves at the expense of moral exemplars survives in mythical "welfare queens" and the poor laws in "welfare reform."[14]

We may speculate that this belief that society is now fallen from grace and thus "demoralized," and that we must impose a neo-Victorian model to remoralize us in the future, will remain a cultural impulse and temptation in the future. The Victorian politician Disraeli spoke then of "the two nations," divided along lines of wealth and poverty. Perhaps in the future the two nations will divide less clearly but no less contentiously between the serious-minded for whom play is a threat to civil order and moral respectability, and the play-minded for whom seriosity is the province of prudish dullards and vindictive ideologues bent on spoiling everyone's fun. Cultural control of fun, and the values associated with fun, will likely be at issue in the "culture wars" of the future. If the play industries and the demand for play keeps expanding, the morally righteous may in waves of panic mount recurrent but unsuccessful crusades to try to reign in the beast of mirth, making themselves into objects of ridicule and enraging and frustrating them further. If cultural persuasion does not turn the historical tide of funning, then the only recourse at that point becomes patently political.

Political Reaction

The party of cultural seriosity, especially in an economic context of scarcity and struggle, might be able to enforce its will through political power. If the pagan din of popular play becomes all the more antinomian and sensational, then the morally responsible can ally with the politically reactionary in a serious effort to shut the carnival down and run the gypsies out of town. Even though such a political agenda would likely be unpopular, those armed with moral certainty and a writ from the police could stop the show. The immediate goal of such a reactionary movement would be to demonize play as a social concept and legitimate activity, and the forms of play they find execrable. Given extensive powers, the party of antiplay could enforce changes in our bad habits of play, and common diversions such as pornography (broadly defined), violent video games, romance novels, rock music channels, and so forth could vanish from many communities.

In the right circumstances, a movement of political reaction could enforce the hegemony of seriosity across the social order. In the presence of economic austerity, for instance, the imposition of compulsive requirements and personal discipline could expand exponentially, justified as a social necessity. The core institution of school might serve as a social model. Progressive ideas about school as a playground and learning as play would disappear. The new model of school would most resemble a prison. The playful aspects of school—courting, conversing, forming cliques, befriending, informal talk with teachers about everything from sex to current events, the fun of finding out neat things—would be replaced by serious requirements learned through regimented drill and personal discipline that punishes individual expression with dress codes and public shamings for misconduct. Like prisons, dress codes become a kind of uniform, and constant shakedowns, isolation, expulsion, and other punishments remind the student inmates that they must serve their time, keep quiet, and eventually either escape or get released. The Dickensian schools of Victorian times emphasized "facts"; the equivalent of that in this scenario would be "tests." Teaching to the test eliminates any silliness about learning for the delight of it, and proves to the educational hierarchy who and who isn't toeing the line in learning official truth. The humanities would emphasize religious and uplifting themes; the social sciences would justify the existing distribution of wealth, status, and power; and the natural sciences would eliminate mention of discredited theories of evolution, the "big bang," and the round Earth. The purpose of school becomes not merely the indoctrination of students into approved orthodoxes and the inculcation of habits of obedience and deference to authority. It is also to restore respect for the hegemony of seriosity: the new message from the principal's office would be *social authority is serious, and no longer tolerates lighthearted fun or playing around*. It would be irrelevant that most students would hate school all the more under such a regimen; they are, after all, supposed to learn that life is

pain. Nor would it matter that school would become the agency of je-
june propaganda that perpetuates a state of ignorance; quite the
contrary, serious ignorance is a cornerstone of such education. The
strength of such learned ignorance is that it is both serious and sanctioned, and negatively, that play is frivolous and dangerous.

This Orwellian agenda could in the worst case lead to dystopian
extremes. A quasi-military regime with expanded police powers and
the technology of surveillance and detection could regiment institutional life into an enforced atmosphere of feet-on-the-floor seriosity.
The "religious" orientation puts the regime on the side of the angels,
doing God's work by instituting moral controls on behavior, and asso-
ciating the regime with sanctification (enforcing prayer, the Pledge
of Allegiance, punishing flag desecrators) and the demonization of
enemies. A neomedieval regime could organize society on the basis of
caste and class, tribal fealties and professional guilds, identifying
the sacral hierarchy that must remain undisturbed. It is already the
case that the top 10–20 percent (in terms of wealth) of the American
population, and roughly the same in other countries such as England, have in many ways successfully seceded from social care; this
"culture of contentment" has such political power, economic protection, and cultural insulation that its privileged denizens, like the
feudal elites ensconced in castles, can effectively ignore the decay of
the rest of society. To the negative freedoms of Roosevelt's Four Freedoms—freedom from want and freedom from fear—these seques-
tered elites may add freedom from care.[15]

A regime of hard-line political reaction would not be entirely grim
and devoid of play. But we can expect that there would be a sharp distinction between good and bad play. Good play would be wholesome
and supportive, such as high school sports and spelling bees. Bad
play would be wicked and dangerous, such as premarital sex and unauthorized Web sites. The distinction would be applied to all endeav-
ors, including drugs. Bad drugs are those sought for the hedonistic
high and participation in acts and groups of rebellion. Good drugs
are those that promote equanimity and docility. The former are de-
monized, and those who are caught using them are severely punished. The latter are prescribed, and those who are troubled are
tranquilized into a smiley face. So users of marijuana and cocaine
are incarcerated, and users of Prozac and Xanax and Luvox are
made placid. Thus such a regime cages potential rebels, and drugs
the unrebellious population with Huxleyian *soma* that promotes servility. The ideology of healthism becomes wedded to a disciplinary
agenda, creating the illusion of living in a pleasantville devoid of

problems and anxieties. It is important for such a regime to take the fun out of play, and to persecute those who dare to have fun with "pleasure drugs." Drugs that promote normalcy contribute to the hegemony of seriosity. We may expect in such a timid new world that all unsanctioned play will go underground, with closet gay and straight lovers meeting in secret, druggies and hackers and gamblers all part of secret groups that the authorities constantly try to destroy. Play becomes the primary enemy of the state.

At its extreme, such an antiplay future could become a kind of reform fascism. But if Heilbroner's prognostication is correct, such a regime might be ideal for withstanding the great tremors of the future. It could offer the organization of society on quasi-military lines and imbue society with a nationalistic and tribal faith. A reform fascism might avoid the extremities of war and genocide, but become a "survival state" that mobilizes all elements of society into a coordinated and subordinated whole. It would likely retain the characteristic dominance of male power, headed by a popular figure who is accorded semidivine status (in the American case, that likely would mean someone with pristine celebrity status, such as a famous and imposing athlete with fervent religious and nativist beliefs). Such a reactionary future would combine the neofeudal elements of a symbolic hierarchy with the postmodern aspects of technological and pharmacological controls. Like the fascisms of old, it would likely display the dramatic force of a bad melodrama, one that is very serious and very strenuous, at its worst in rites of purification. But any future fascism can be sure to be very hard on play. Nothing alarms the fascist mind more than not being taken seriously, and not taking the world seriously. There is something impure about playfulness, and suspect about being laughed at. (Hitler and the Nazis, we may recall, were maddened by their fantasy that throughout the program of annihilation the Jews were secretly laughing at them.) So we might expect that an American fascism would include a war on play, reforming the institutions of play to allow only serious play that supports the regime, and expanding to the node the surveillance of the play attitude that so threatens the ardent seriosity of the state. The fascist mentality is not content until the last smile has been wiped off the face of someone who doesn't take the new order seriously.

PLAYING THE PALACE OF THE FUTURE

Happily, we can state that there are good reasons to think that the dystopian extremes of antiplay will not triumph in the near future.

The historical developments described earlier are powerful social forces with influence over people's lives that will likely expand in the future. If that is to be the case, then we need to speculate as to what a future play world might look like, and indeed even attempt to imagine what civilization of, say, the year 2084 might look like if play continues to expand as a practice and value.

Increased Economic Growth

Even if we admit that the exponential growth of the world economy cannot continue without exhausting resources, it is still likely that significant segments of the world population will enjoy continuing prosperity. The world of the twenty-first century will no doubt experience difficult environmental and population problems that will mitigate economic expansion and the wide distribution of available wealth. But the triumph of the market economy will continue to create demand for pleasurable experiences. Even in struggling Third World countries (not to mention poor regions of the West, such as inner cities in old American cities or the rural Southwest), the desire for more follows the irrepressible logic of consumerism. Modern economies are perpetuated by advertisements heralding the good life, and this propagated strategy of desire creates ever anew our thirst for novelty and new stimuli. Even if we admit and enforce limits to growth, the hope for the good life defined as prosperity and play will continue to flourish.[16]

If there is merit to the argument that economic growth in a market economy promotes individual liberty, it will be difficult for social authorities to abate the demand for free expression. That includes not only economic choice and political liberty, but also cultural play. In the future, popular culture will continue to serve poorly as an agent of social control as well as an agent of diversity and even rebellion. Virtually all economies and polities will be put in the position of becoming leisure states, forced to allow economic innovation and political liberty because the cultural force of consumers cannot abide servility and obedience, not to mention poverty. In the future, we may well see economic hope decline as environmental strain and recessions develop, and also see political hope decline as political systems fail to meet rising demand and deal with the eclipse of seriosity. Instead, we may see these replaced by cultural hope born of frustration with economic and political life and satisfying fun in play life.

This is not to say that economic life will not continue. But if a modicum of wealth and social choice remains in large populations, their commitment to a lifetime of labor and the value of accumulation may be superceded by other interests. If in a labor society the core dynamic is to eliminate labor costs, then the sense of irrelevance to the system will lead people to find meaning and purpose elsewhere. People at work see the mutual commitment of employer and employee disappear, and there is less necessity for everyone to work and search for something more rewarding to do. The future may see a great deal more of voluntary joblessness, migratory and career switches in jobs, and for many, perpetual underemployment. The price of labor may become too high for both employers and employees.

Following the play attitude engendered by cultural experience, people may increasingly bring to work a ludenic spirit. With e-trading easily available to everyone with money to bet, playing the stock market and related markets (commodities, options, currencies, and the like) may become more prevalent. Since many people enjoy the risk, we may expect that they will think "investing is fun."[17] This is one new way that people will become self-employed. It may also be the modal form of gambling, superceding the traditional forms of the gambling industry. If people figure out that the odds are against them at the roulette table or racetrack or video poker parlor, they may begin to think the odds of playing the market are better. Future gamblers will not study racing forms and poker odds, but rather the percentages of options trading and technology stocks. And if "business civilization" and the labor society decline, this may augur the rise of a new barter economy. People who have visited the open-air markets of cities such as London and Paris, or the bazaars of Third World countries, know that many people enjoy the give-and-take and haggle of bartering over a sale. Bartering is fun, since both sides to the negotiated deal are engaged in economic play. They are dealing with the brute fact of barter, and are amused by the art of the deal ("Let's trade"), rather than the institutional facts of market systems ("private property," "corporation," "stockbrokering"). Our acquiescence of the latter may erode if we can freely engage in the former, and find it more enjoyable.[18] Indeed, Internet sites such as eBay put barter on-line, wherein millions of traders can deal for everything imaginable. (Perhaps the re-emergence of a barter economy worldwide brings us full circle, supporting the retrospective view that Stone Age humans were not so much hunters and gatherers as they were traders: the art of the deal for flints on England's Ridgeway drew barterers from as far away as Germany and Spain.)

It may also be the case that people in the future, at least the fortunate ones, will no longer make a clear distinction between work and play. One observes high-tech companies in the Silicon Valleys of the world and finds that the older distinctions of organizational hierarchy, the division of labor defined in job descriptions, and the earnest attitude of work have vanished. Instead we see a roughly egalitarian and fluid organization, cooperative and changeable effort in groups, and a relaxed and playful attitude. Perhaps the creativity of some of these firms comes from the flow of ideas and innovations that such an atmosphere encourages. It is true that such companies consist of highly educated professionals used to working and playing together, and that we are a long way from sweatshops in Honduras and Indonesia. But such economic organizations could serve as a model for the future that many other firms could emulate. A future of creative work and productive play combined may mean we have to invent new terms to name the new activity: "workplay," "playwork," "leisurework," "ludenic labor," and so on. Perhaps this is an indication that we are moving from the age of the "organization person" to the "unorganized person," the latter being the mobile and multiskilled worker who expects the workday and the workplace to be flexible and congenial; if it isn't, she or he is quite capable of moving on—and willing to do so. A world of workplayers would be latter-day gypsies, recast as cosmopolitan transit loungers who move from project to project, continent to continent, the ultimate hireling. The global market culture makes for an astonishingly mobile workforce, many of whom enjoy the travel and adventure and challenge of jet-set piecework. The global economy and transnational corporation will be paralleled by a roaming force of specialized workers who keep their bags packed and their passport up to date.

For most people in the new economy, many of the same realities of making do and living with the grind of work will still apply. But in the future it may be that their key labor issue is the unequal distribution of play. The issues of wages, benefits, and working conditions will still apply, but the universality of the play culture will impel them to demand the time and opportunity to play. Rather than Luddite revolts to save jobs or conserve technology, we may see ludenic revolts that demand the right to have fun. Third World countries will continue to have cheap labor, but that labor will increasingly see the advent of the play culture close by: movie theaters, cable TV, gambling casinos, resort towns, touring companies, bars and bistros, restaurants and franchise foods, theme parks, and so on. Labor agitation will center on acquiring the means to gain access to the

wonderful world of play. Indeed, when unemployment or other economic troubles emerge, governments may find it necessary to provide people with "play chits" that give them access to play. Rather
than risk risings by the disgruntled and deprived, social peace is
bought by giving them passes to shows and tours and all the delights
and diversions the play world has invented. The barrios of Latin
America might be made quiescent by wiring them for cable television. The world economy may not be able to provide high-paying jobs
or full benefits anymore, but it may be able to stabilize the laboring
classes by making sure they have access to fun.

The economic world of 2084 might have several features, some of
which we would recognize and some we would not. If the entertainment economy continues to grow, then we might surmise that more
and more people will spend lots more money and time at play. If
fewer people are needed to do the world's work, then we will have to
find ways to spend money and pass time. But this assumes that the
consumer economy will continue on its current course. There could
be a significant revulsion against the philistinism of the consumer
habit, or an economic downturn or even catastrophe that effectively
ends the consumer habit for the many have-nots. In that event, 2084
could witness new forms of play that do not require a lot of money.
People could engage in environmental, archaeological, or scientific
play, taking time off to restore a forest, or dig up Indian mounds, or
study rare species. People could turn to religious or philosophical
quests, taking pilgrimages to holy places or joining a cult or fraternity committed to thought and meditation. Others could form groups
committed to some value, such as sensual abandon or the simple
communal life free of technology or gypsy wandering or the worship
of nature (or, to come full circle again, as in the earliest civilizations,
to the making and quaffing of beer). People may find creative ways to
play that do not require money or an industry for them to have fun,
and with serendipitous consequences: hikers and climbers and bird-
ers and other nature lovers may save the environment.

The triumph of play as a social principle might even mean that the
future world economy is organized on a different basis rather than
systemic market exchange and the ethic of accumulation. The contemporary basis of economic life is based in the myth that market
values are the criterion of truth, and that economy is the decisive and
ultimate perspective on how the world works and what makes people go. But this is the view of those committed to the rule of the *numerate*, that counting up who has what in terms of monetary or
proprietary units constitutes heroic achievement and social value.

This is an "accountant's view of the world," numbering everything and everyone as to accountable worth. What might emerge instead is an "economy of happiness."[19] An economy of happiness would be committed to making people happy. If they conclude that play is a happier activity than earnest work, then an economy could be organized on that basis. What this might look like requires Utopian speculation, but it certainly would define the principle of the greatest happiness for the greatest number in terms of maximizing the amount and quality of fun the great majority of people are having, or could have if they want. Suffice it to say here that this would be an economy much different than our current system.

Political Cosmopolis

Long ago, the great pioneer filmmaker D. W. Griffith made a startling prediction: historical innovation was changing who people regarded as national heroes. In the past, warriors were so exalted, but they now (1921) were being superceded by industrialists. The advent of the motion picture was going to change that: as people awoke to the power of popular art, the artist would replace the industrialist as the popular hero of the many.[20] At the height of the power of Nazi Germany and Stalinist Russia, the aforementioned Harold D. Lasswell foresaw the emergence of "garrison states": the democratic and autocratic states had been dominated by businessmen, who were specialists on bargaining ("Let's make a deal"); now these were replaced by soldiers, who were specialists on violence ("Let's fight till you surrender or die").[21] Following Griffith, perhaps what we are seeing now is the emergence of artists who will assume political leadership roles and heroic endeavor ("Let me entertain you"). Businesspeople are committed to the rule of the numerate, and soldiers to the rule of force, both earnest forms of domination. Even though political control of the economy and political control of territories and populations will continue to be important in the future, it may be that such agendas will be amended or superceded by a more popular and accessible endeavor, realizing the agenda of the leisure state. In that eventuality, artists who are specialists in entertainment will possess the skills to communicate their commitment to play, and to the projects of an economy of happiness and a polity that creates the conditions of social tolerance and cultural vivacity.

The task for the political artists of the future will be formidable, for much of the political alienation and cynicism we have described will persist, given the operational ethos of the news media and the popular assumptions about the squalor and venality of political life.

Future historians, attempting to explain the present, will have to come to grips with the question of why the millennial period had such a robust economy and vital culture but such petty and mean politics. Perhaps there is merit in the view that people are turned off by politics because it is no fun. Whereas the global economy at least claims to be inclusive and "lifting all boats," and the popular culture is in principle open to all comers, politics has a forbidding and exclusive quality. Divided into warring factions and parties, political life is bickering and intolerant, hampered by win-lose/either-or/us-them thinking, and worst of all, the political class takes itself seriously. To restore interest, future political artists will have to move politics away from conflictuality to conviviality. Rather than viewing politics as a rather unfunny farce, they should invite us to see politicking as a comedy of manners. Farce gives people the sense that no one is competent enough to run things, whereas comedy of manners stresses that despite the gap between manners and morals, and the inevitable appearance of hypocrisy, situations can play out with endings that are both funny and happy. A new play attitude featuring both sophistication and inclusion could move the future from crabbiness to conversation, from intolerance to tolerance, from disengagement to engagement, from childishness to maturity, and from petty seriosity to joyful conviviality.

By stressing the mannerly dimension, politics in the future could acquire a higher level of courtesy and decorum, and a broader breadth of perspective. The farcical view sees politics only as a contest, agonistic play stressing the adversarial tangle that in the view of observers and commentators always deteriorates into buffoonery and burlesque. Politics here is only an "argument culture" in which rational debate and thoughtful proposals are shouted down by activists for whom "the fight's the thing" or are destroyed by clever media imagery and innuendo, and the public quits the bullies' street fight in disgust. The political contestants who narrow politics to eye-gouging fights simply wind up glorifying aggression and making politics seem all the more farcical.[22] Political etiquette and classy magnanimity would be enhanced if the political strata and public could regard politics as empathic play. Comedies of manners highlight human failings but elicit understanding of the characters involved and the complex ambiguity of human motives and situations. A political comedy of manners would elicit empathic play, favoring those with a touch of class, reintroducing the delights of play into the overserious and agonistic politics of the present.

The agonistic world of politics comes to be regarded as farce because it deteriorates into a closed entropic system. Such a system evolves into a self-perpetuating and exclusive group that excludes innovation and solutions, transforming contests into rituals that institutionalize plotting and bickering but avoid both change and commitment. Such a system becomes impervious to the external world outside its carefully constructed monad, and increasingly becomes devoted to celebrations of self-reference and self-importance. Its internal agonistic habit contributes to a sense of separation from, and conflict with, the always threatening external world. It is entropic because it is closed to adaptation and revitalizing inclusion and fresh results. It achieves consensual validation through the "groupthink" of a caste system, devout observances of ceremonies, and high seriosity.[23] The elite systems of late eighteenth-century Paris, early twentieth-century Saint Petersburg, and late twentieth-century Washington all displayed these characteristics.

Despite their self-image as sophisticated and urbane, these capitals were in fact parochial and insular. Such systems ironically ensure stability by excluding vitality, which makes them a worthy subject of farce. (It is no accident that in late twentieth-century America, Washington politics were a prime subject of comedy.) The introduction of vitality would require a more cosmopolitan attitude that addresses problems but reduces seriosity through self-deprecating humor. This suggests the perspective of a comedy of manners: politics is fun, and funny, because all human foibles, especially self-deception and affectation, are exposed for our delectation and amusement. In this way, politics is not to be regarded as a morality play wherein we condemn the tragic gap between manners and morals, but rather as an object of light comedy This view means, in Ben Jonson's words, that we "sport with human follies, not with crimes," and regard the less than pristine behavior of people as laughable rather than condemnable. This bemused and genial attitude looks upon the human comedy with the puckish thought of what fools these mortals be, and the worldly wise expectation that this, too, shall pass.

This larger view of politics lets us see what is going on at any moment as part of the passing cavalcade of human life in all its colorful variety. If people in the future can see themselves as part of a political *cosmopolis*, perhaps they can adhere to a sagacious and capacious view of things, as part of the endless human struggle to civilize politics. But this requires a motive for participation other than the common desire to either do well or do good by political activity. The former act out of self-interest, hoping for gain for one's self or advantage for one's affiliation. The latter act out of moral concern, hoping for higher standards of political conduct or, at the puritan extreme, for the imposition of solemn seriosity and punitive controls across society. But neither approach breathes new life into a moribund system, since the former approach has a stake in bilking the system as it exists, and the latter imposes yet more strictures and rules to further bind the system to legalistic or academic governance. The quest for advantage or the imposition of rules creates the conditions for farcical situations, such as the deadlock of competing interests or attempts at enforcing iron rules on a diverse and recalcitrant populace. Neither approach introduces an element of vitality that might open the system and reverse entropy.

This might be done by the entry into the system of those who participate because it is play. Cosmopolites who see politics as a comedy of manners engage in political activity devoid of an agenda of self-interest or moral rule making, but with the heart of an amateur, playing politics for the pure hell of it. Their larger view of the political world is both historical and philosophical, so they have no illusions about its dealing and double-dealing, and its imperviousness to moral crusades. All they hope for is that it can be more civilized, harkening back to the tradition of skeptical humanism exemplified by Machiavelli and Montaigne and Shakespeare.[24] This tradition is skeptical of both assertions of vast power and strictures of moral duty, since both can lead to disaster; and is humane enough to admit that the world of power will never be conquered by the world of love, but can hope that it can be made more civil and less serious by introducing revitalizing participants into the system whose sense of adventure and good humor can bring new life and hope into the deadening rituals of power. Politics is a "game without end," to be sure, but if change can be introduced from the outside by those willing to play, the game will not atrophy and become marginal because of its inability to change, and it will let in those whose conviviality and verve bring refreshing play into the system.[25]

The future politics of many systems will depend upon the degree of play that elites allow and incorporate. The current regime of China, for instance, could have been brighter if elites had found ways to bring dissenting youth into the system, rather than killing and jailing them. That dreary and insulated party-state is in danger of fearing, and thus crushing, youthful forces that would revitalize the system, thus ensuring eventual systemic collapse that includes revenge on the old regime's oppressive nature. The United States faces the entropic problem of nonparticipation: many people sense that the system has no interest in their well-being, doesn't invite their participation, and has devolved into a self-perpetuating but devitalized capital.[26] Political atrophy can have consequences as severe as oppression, in that the system cannot survive widespread contempt for its practices and disregard for its commands. Governmental centers cannot hold if their grip is too tight or loose, since "play in the system" finds expression elsewhere. The state withers away from the disease of terminal seriosity.

In the new century, we may wonder if we are witnessing another great transformation. All over the world, new and vital elites are becoming connected. They locate themselves as at home in the world, identifying with global enterprises and universal values. They extend themselves in communication with like-minded people virtually everywhere. The flow of their lives is in the cosmopolitan and interrelated worlds of technology, economics, and culture as they transact worldwide. Computer scientists and financial managers and entertainers and journalists and so on are all part of the new strata of the world elite. From Beijing to São Paulo to Chicago to Bonn to Nairobi to Moscow, we may expect these new worldly elites to feel confident and future-oriented, since they are competent at what they do, doing well, and having a hell of a lot of fun. They all will speak the same universal languages, technoese, financialese, and popese. And they likely will share a contempt for the local, the traditional, and the old fogeys who have always run things. In this attitude, they will regard politics and politicians with contempt, and invent clever ways to circumvent and defeat the efforts of local political elites who interfere with their global perspectives and identifications. This development obviously will create the conditions for real conflicts between struggling political elites attempting to enforce local control and their most talented and connected citizens determined to reach the outside world they associate with knowledge, riches, and fun. If these new classes associate politics with archaic and hidebound arrangements that attempt to stem the tide of the future, then politics as the previous century knew it—based in national or subnational locations, with knowledge and communication controlled by parochial political elites, and identifications defined as loyal patriotism and particularistic values—will likely become increasingly marginal to the exercise of economic and cultural power. "Arrogant capitals" will become humbled as they watch helplessly the flow of power toward international corporations, communications and Internet systems, and cultural experience.

For this reason, there is now speculation about the emergence of a "postpolitical" community that hopes to retain the best in local traditions and habits but transcend the stupid and vicious pettiness and chauvinism that characterizes so many political locales. There is the potential in some places for the rise of "the digital citizen," people who hope for a moral civil society that overcomes ideological and tribal divisions, believe that technology and market systems are a force for good, and put much faith in the power of rational discussion and the spread of communication to make politics more palatable. Digital citizens are not alienated cynics, but rather optimistic and participatory, hoping for a new politics freed of cant and eager for technologically engendered discussion. Skeptics may doubt that politics can be transformed and matured by everyone having an e-mail address, but the existence of such networks of like-minded people is a refreshing sign that the politics of the future might just be different. If so, it will be because digital citizens find it playful: they choose to participate in political "sites" and engage in political discussions that are fun. If it isn't fun, they, like everyone else enamored with the digital world, simply move to another site that is.[27]

The revitalization of politics would be enhanced and matured if it were no longer considered a social arena of agonistic play, which may be a characteristically male undertaking, and advanced instead into an activity of empathic play, which may be more feminine in character. Politics could be made more mannerly, and more fun, if it became in the future more courteous, delicate, and elegant. If *agon* is a male approach stressing contestation, then the metaphor of political life is too often war, the roughest and deadliest form of human play. *Empathos* might gentle politics down, since the metaphor suggested here is nurture. Nurturing the "public household" brings cooperative and convivial imagery, including the cultivation of gardens. An empathic feminine sensibility in politics might not end contestation, but it would change the rules and practices from win-lose contests to win-win projects. Most of all, politics would be enriched by female fun, which would replace male charisma with charm, male argument with sensibility, and male incivility with civility. If women are actually more biologically and psychologically secure than men, then their political sense of humor and comedic empathy might make politics less imbued with pinched male seriosity and more infused with expansive female lightness.[28] (Models abound: the politicized women in Aristophanes' *Lysistrata* are enjoying themselves immensely.) The feminization of politics would have a bisociative effect, since the formerly incongruous presence of the feminine and female wit would induce creative responses, and in the process make politics a lot more fun for all.[29]

Cultural Festivity

It has been recently hypothesized that the great divisions of the future will be cultural, featuring the "clash of civilizations." These civilizations are ancient and rooted in such basic identifications as region, religion, language, ethnicity, and "race," indeed all those things that make them cohere as a culture. The West will be at odds with civilizations such as the Confucian, Hindu, Slavic-Orthodox, and Islamic. Differences in basic values and beliefs undermine ideas about a spreading world culture or universal civilization. Western culture has permeated the world only at a superficial level. For the foreseeable future, these civilizations will be at odds, and Western political, economic, and cultural imperialism will be resisted and resented.[30]

This futuristic vision is at odds with the thesis that mass communications and popular culture will penetrate into the non-Western world and transform its peoples into citizens of a universal civilization who participate in a common culture of humankind. These two scenarios are not the only two prospects. On the one hand, the particularistic aspects of civilizations (and the varying cultures that constitute them) will continue to color their view of the West and the spread of popular culture. But on the other hand, they are not windowless monads. They are not immune to the impact of the "McWorld" to which they have increasing access and adapt to their own particular way of life. The future may witness many variations on resisting, blending, and uniting cultural habits and practices. At least a large and growing portion of humankind will know about the larger world, the languages of pop Esperanto it speaks (such as popular music), and the universal values (such as choice and leisure) that it entails. As this popular knowledge spreads, many people will feel psychic tugs and strains, and many may experience the kinds of protean changes we have described.

We may agree that individuals and cultures everywhere will feel the conflict between their local traditions and the world culture. An important component of this conflict will be in the area of play. Virtually all local cultures have traditions of cultural festivity in a communal or national setting. So everyone has some intuitive knowledge of the fun of play in a festive milieu. Perhaps the great cultural conflict of the future will be over the wisdom of participating in the cultural festivity of the play world that has appeared from elsewhere. The world culture spreads the means of play, to be sure, but more importantly it spreads the *idea* of play. If the play world does expand into most all places around the globe, it will be because of the gradual legitimation of a *cultural cosmopolis*, wherein cultural authority shifts to those institutions and symbolic figures who promote play as a cosmopolitan value and practice. If one plays in settings and with means provided by the play world, that means that one identifies with a value associated with the world civilization and not the local culture. The Confucian civilization may have enduring power, but the kids rockin' at the Hard Rock Cafe in Hong Kong, the surfers breaking through Net restrictions in Shanghai, and even the hamburgers sold at the McDonald's in Beijing introduce cosmopolitan play into an enduring culture. In a sense, the introduction of such cultural innovations becomes the most difficult to resist, since it is no direct threat to the political and economic system and may seem harmless enough. But it also often has a snowball effect, with the spread of popular play and the demand for more growing rapidly. Superficial play has a way of propagating, becoming more important and widespread than anyone could have dreamed. How long a country such as China can retain the mix of one-party political rule, free market Stalinism, and controlled cultural innovation remains to be seen.

Play may well become a powerful force for future change because it has by now acquired the status of a myth. A myth is not a falsity or tall tale, but rather a symbolic story that gives poetic meaning and direction to cultural life. Myths speak great truths with universal application for that culture. Cultures may have founding myths, heroic myths, and so forth; they may also have more abstract and transcultural myths such as the modern myths of work, progress, and happiness, what have been called "ontological myths" expressing some great truth to which we should all be directed and to which we are entitled. It may be that the modern myths of work and progress have decayed, and that people have more difficulty believing in the nobility of work and the inevitability of progress.[31] But there does appear to be a future for the myth of happiness. There is and will be great resonance to Jefferson's felicitous and famous phrase "the pursuit of happiness." We suggest here that the ontological myth of the coming era will be pursuing happiness, and that the cosmopolitan world culture will tend to define happiness as the willingness and ability to have fun.

If we are indeed in a "liminal" age, in transition from the modern world to something vaguely prognosticated as the "postmodern" age (what is this new age "pre-?"), old myths may become difficult to sustain. (The term introduced above—"postintellectualism"—may be more incisive: when intellect is superceded by intuition, whatever makes us happy is true.) If work in the future no longer includes the rewards of workmanship or the predictability of security, and if progress dissipates into clashes of ancient allegiances and conflicts redefined as "civilizations," then the locus of hope will be what is worth pursuing: happy times, happy talk, and happy relations. If many people find the literal world unsatisfying, they may seek satisfaction in nonliteral worlds that they define as the places to pursue happiness. If happiness is to become the key world cultural myth of the future, then the culturo-logic of the quest leads to the activity that is viewed as providing the most potential happiness: play. The fair times of memory will be the instances of extraordinary fun, the precious times of the present will be those that become fun, and the horizon of the future promises the pursuit of fun. Play becomes a myth to live by, acquiring the ontological status of an ethic and a purpose: play is by nature good.

In the future, then, the captivating myth of play may encourage us to define ourselves as humankind the player, *homo ludens*, over and against other social identities such as "political man" or "economic man." In a sense, this new (and very old) myth of human meaning and destiny is a poetic rather than pragmatic definition of our being. Here is an *aesthetic* self-definition: rather than *homo politicus* or *homo faber*, we are closer to *homo poeta*, humankind the artist.[32] If this myth prevails in the future, then the core of our being and where we live will be at play.

The myth of play transforms the pursuit of happiness into a *cultural enthymeme*. Biologist Richard Dawkins coined the now popular term "meme," and as a social metaphor it has acquired wide usage to denote "contagious ideas," "units of meaning," "cultural replicators," "cultural software," and the like.[33] But as the term is used, "meme" connotes a viral or epidemiological process of cultural evolution and innovation. It is perhaps more useful to use the wider Aristotelian term "enthymeme," from the logical syllogism in which one of the premises is implict or understood but not stated, but it advances the argument or practice. A cultural enthymeme implies a myth that is assumed as the implicit premise, and proceeds to act upon that myth through activity. The logic of play proceeds from the myth of happiness to ludenic actions. From the implicit premise "Play is good," the injunction play animates attitude and attention, identifying play ("This is play") and inviting action ("Let's play").

We may hypothesize here that the cultural enthymeme of happiness manifest in play will be a major mythic force in the future. In the world civilization that will exist as a cosmopolitan counterpoise, play will be a delightful way to enjoy experience associated with the world culture. Perhaps many people with some degree of access will be able to live in both worlds, working and parenting and so on in the local culture and escaping into play as a participant in the world culture. The Islamic urban professionals who go to spas where they can drink and gamble, the frugal Japanese bourgeoisie who jet to supermalls to shop till they drop, youth cultures everywhere that share music and dance and popular art—all are entering the cosmopolitan play world without leaving the local culture to which they regularly belong. The protean selves of the future may learn how to "shapeshift" into players who can enter and leave the play world at ease, returning to local seriosity and moral strictures after stints of delicious play elsewhere. But people everywhere will understand the rules of playing in the cosmopolitan culture, without unduly sacrificing their identity with, and "normal" life in, the local culture or civilization. Their time in the play world will be remembered as an enchanted "oasis of happiness" wherein they gave themselves over to festivity.

It is in these festive experiences that the playful attitude could have its cumulative effect, for people take home with them memories of the *festive spirit*. Local cultures usually have holidays or other periods set aside for festivity. But the world civilization offers access to festivity at all times, if one can afford it and gain access to it. The cosmopolitan world is creating a carnival culture in which it is legitimate to play all the time. Local cultures may or may not resist the serious inroads of global capitalism and universal political values, but the play attitude and the festive spirit are both more ephemeral and more insidious. "All play," wrote Eugen Fink, "magically produces a play world. . . . The play world is an imaginary dimension . . . an enigmatic realm that is not nothing, and yet is nothing real."[34] This ephemeral realm forever tantalizes those who have been enchanted by its lures and promises, and lingers in memory and hope as an experience worth remembering and anticipating. The very ephemeral status of the play world makes it all the more fantastic and therefore more alluring. If our local lives tend toward the mundane, the "nothing real" of play is calling us to a place where we can exult in the sheer lightness of being. At its most fantastic level, we can imagine ourselves in play worlds in which we are mortal gods in a secular heaven.[35]

The influx and diffusion of play experiences raises the concomitant possibility of the persistence and promotion of play values. If play is an exercise in self-expression and aesthetic experience, then a return to the quotidian suggests insidious questions: Why can't we have more play? Can we not have oases of happiness right here in River City (or Kabul, or Nanking, or Managua)? Such an attitudinal innovation gives credence to all sorts of desires and demands concerning the availability of play. And, since play is in some measure an expression of freedom and exhilaration, it becomes easy to associate play with economic and political freedom. The world civilization of global capitalism and political democracy brings with it the prosperity and liberty that lets us play. (The Eastern European countries under spartan communist rule, such as East Germany, were well aware of the absence of both prosperity and liberty, and also of play: they could sometimes pick up Western European television and radio advertising promising the delights of play through a product or service.) The myth of the enchanting fulfillments of play gives associative support to the desire to create the wealth to afford play, and for the liberty to choose play. Traditions of local play may be lost or amended with the introduction of the industries and technologies that provide play (e.g., gambling, movies, restaurant chains, televised sports), but for many people this appears not to be too high a price to pay. If many cultures and civilizations around the world become blends of the world civilization and the local habitat, this will include negotiating the role of play in their lives.

In the future, then, we may have multiple sources of cultural festivity. As a cultural enthymeme, play may have a powerful influence on attitudes and actions almost everywhere. If the competitive forces of economic expansion and political democracy become widespread, then play will acquire even more poignancy and urgency as a respite from new and demanding forms of seriosity. We may speculate that in some places, a crisis might develop wherein the choice between activities of seriosity and activities of play become competitive. Do we stay at the office, or hit the links? Why continue working, when I have the means to play? Is the economic or political game worth the candle? If we can swing it, why don't we spend *all* our time at play? Is there some reason why life can't be fun all the time? Can we be festive people at play, and can every occasion be a festival? If these basic questions arise, some will begin to speculate on a radical question: what would a play civilization look like?

THE FESTIVE CIVILIZATION

If the cultural enthymeme of happiness through play expanded to the node, what would society look like? To paraphrase Hobbes, how is a play society possible? We wish to conclude our inquiry with some Utopian thoughts on the possibility and nature of a civilization based on play. Can we imagine a way of life in the future in which play is the primary form of social interaction? Most of the readers of this book live in societies in which play is ancillary, an interlude between the routines of the serious life, and the primary activities expected of most of us are laborious and responsible. But what if the world were turned upside down, and we found ourselves living in a new civilization devoted to play? What would it be like, and what would we do?

Since such a civilization is virtually unprecedented on any large scale, it is impossible to know for certain whether a play world is feasible or even imaginable. Some things do seem clear. A society devoted to play would be committed to moving from the pursuit of happiness to the *condition* of happiness. Some of the mythic injunctions of previous societies—"Be pious!," "Be useful!," "Be rich!," "Be powerful!," or "Be famous!"—are superceded by the admonition "Be happy!" Both human motives and human ethics direct our desires and norms toward the goal of human happiness. In the history of social thought, this would continue the trend away from the classical view of humanity as creatures who seek virtue, and the early modern view of humanity as seekers of rational self-interest, toward the more recent idea of humanity as pursuers of happiness. The philosophical school named utilitarianism was aimed at the perhaps Utopian goal of widespread human felicity, the greatest happiness for the greatest number. They hedged on whether happiness was possible with only hedonistic pleasures, and whether the pursuit of any pleasure was permissible, arguing that through education and refinement, people would choose the "higher pleasures," at the highest, the life of the mind. But this makes happiness a matter of taste, and for many, a modicum of hedonic pleasures will do.

Implicit in this Utopian view is that what makes us happiest, and thus forms the basis of the full flowering of *homo ludens*, is play. The philosopher Frederich Schiller long ago maintained that "Man plays only when he is in the full sense of the word a man, and he is only wholly Man when he is playing."[36] This aesthetic view seems to eliminate infantile play among adults as childish and tragic play as self-destructive. The regressive play of drunken students or the suicidal play of artistic excess among rock singers promote evils, not happiness. We may expect that future societies committed to the play ethic will attempt to moderate play from destructive excess and direct it toward social festivity that is acceptable. The difficulty no doubt will be determining who decides which forms of play are acceptable and which are not. Once the principle of individual happiness is established, it becomes harder to dictate what is good play and what is bad play, and to forbid choosing that deemed bad. Once this is dictated, we are again in the realm of social engineering of play, imbuing it with a serious social function such as education or control, as we mentioned with Huxley's *Brave New World*.

This will be a major consideration in societies committed to play, since play is dangerous. Nietzsche's famous distinction between Apollonian and Dionysian play is still relevant. Apollonian play directs us toward the higher pleasures of intellectual and artistic play. This kind of play promotes learning and inquiry, the play of the mind and the joy of contemplation and intelligent conversation, and the ecstasy of discovery. Since Aristotle, intellectuals have found, not surprisingly, that intellectual pleasures are the highest. A society trying to promote socially acceptable play might emphasize the "play of the mind" as good fun. But more troublesome is the lure of Dionysian play, with the search for the limits of experience, the fulfillment of desire, and the emphasis on physical ecstasy and erotic play. It has been the tradition to regard Apollonian pleasures as higher and more acceptable than Dionysian ones, but in the future, as now, that may be difficult to enforce. In many traditions, the festive spirit of revelry allows periodic outbursts of mirth and gaiety. What we have little precedent for is the attitude that life can be one continuous party, and that there is no moral or economic reason why Dionysian revels cannot go on without hindrance. What had been confined to carnival time or social groups such as decadent elites or bohemian subcultures becomes a social norm, a state of permanent festivity. Freed from constraints and necessities, many people could engage in long periods of fun, abandoning a sense of guilt for enjoying themselves, and a sense of anxiety for ignoring ambition and acquisition. Whatever we may think of them, the fun people of the future will not be driven by the older devils of moral rectitude or economic success.

In the driven present, we may find such people, then as now, shockingly irresponsible. But recall that we are engaged in social forecasting: if the legitimacy as well as the availability of play triumphs in the future, we may expect people to engage in play longer, more intently, and with less inhibition. It has long been one of the functions of social authorities, figuratively speaking, to take the punch bowl away before the party gets out of hand. But in a festive society, the provision of happiness becomes a primary function, and thus, interfering with play runs counter to social myth. Hence social authorities may be expected to keep the punch bowl full and let the good times roll. If play attains the status of a basic human good, then the "fun morality" of having a good time becomes unarguable. Play could be extolled as the quintessence of human expression, something done for its own sake, for the joy of it, and without ulterior motive or serious intent.[37] In the future, social conservatives in festive societies may find themselves defending play and festivity as values worth conserving against the encroachments of earnestness and the dreariness of useful industry and responsible citizenry.

If a festive society is possible, it will be because people discover that play has its own kind of truth.[38] We may speculate on what a healthy *play self* might look like. Such people are obviously willing and able to be festive, and define the meaning of life in terms of enjoyment. They think people at their best when they don't take themselves too seriously, and cultivate an exquisite and boundless sense of humor and goodwill. The play self is able to balance the desire for Apollonian play and Dionysian play, exercising the goods of the mind and the goods of the body in sheer enjoyment, and recognizing that solving an intellectual question or sophisticated conversation is as much fun as physical pleasures or the jocularity of leisurely discourse. The play self includes a well-developed aesthetic sensibility, believing that art is the furthest reach of play, and that the art of living and the art of appreciation should both be cultivated. Those who define the meaning of life as enjoyment concentrate on living well as opposed to acquiring power, wealth, or fame. The goods of seriosity involve the direct striving for ends, whereas living well in a condition of play is an end in itself. Life is regarded as too important to take seriously.

A festive society would clearly have a different attitude toward *employment*. In societies committed to earnest endeavor, employment involve the division of labor. One is employed in classwork or housework or jobwork, and labor is rewarded in some way or another. But employment can also mean other ways to utilize time and energy. People can be employed in activities other than work. A festive society would include large numbers of people who do not have to work for a living, or do not care to work hard or long; their orientations and interests are elsewhere, in activities that are fun. They would be employed in activity other than labor, some of which might be deemed useful: environmental or animal assistance, social volunteering, archeological digging, and so on. Many others may be frankly devoted to festivity, but feel quite adequately employed in arranging dinner parties, attending foodfests, leading an active and varied sex life, and touring wineries and brew pubs. And some are self-employed in contemplation, the feast of ideas, and the mirth of inquiry. Finally, a few may find enjoyment in idleness. It could even be the case that those who exist in graceful idleness are subjects of great admiration and emulation, since idleness may be regarded as the ultimate act of festive play. Anyone can do something; it takes a certain kind of genius to master the art of doing nothing.

At its worst, a festive society could deteriorate into the frivolous and languid, devoid of meaningful accomplishment achieved through serious effort. Play may be inadequate as a means of human happiness, and certainly of aspiration. At its best, such a society could greatly broaden the scope and depth of human happiness. People would feel freer, more sensitive, and open to the novel and pleasurable than ever before. Much that has been dreadful and boring in human existence could be livened up by making it playful. School could revitalize itself by remembering its Greek origins as play, abandoning its routines of seriosity, and making learning fun. Eureka! would be the cry regularly heard from every schoolroom, and festivity would reign (Marshall McLuhan once suggested that all higher education should be conducted in pubs, putting academic discussion in a convivial setting). Kids might cease to hate school because it would enhance rather than interfere with their education. School conducted as playful inquiry would stimulate rather than kill inquisitiveness.[39] The point of departure for school should not be the staid tedium of the classroom, but the vibrant and anarchic exuberance of recess on the playground.

Perhaps the most notable and arresting feature of a festive society would be its vitality. Festive people enjoy the celebration of life, and find much to celebrate. The cultural enthymeme of play enjoins the recurrent and frequent flourish of celebratory occasions. Since such occasions are happy times, they become the core event of social life. A festive society cannot rid the world of everyday requirements and the inevitability of doomsday, but it can enjoy merry interludes that are cause for rejoicing. (The festive would agree with Auntie Mame that life is a banquet, and most poor suckers are starving to death.) The spirit of festivity continuously revitalizes social life, wherein the renewal of merry hearts gives impetus to the desire for novelty, the love of sensibility, and the exercise of liberty. Other societies may be characterized by the stilted comforts of artifice or the urges toward

domination and destruction, and eliminate as much of the celebratory and carefree as they can. Social artifices can become phony, and
the will to power can become morbid and deadly. But the truly festive have no need to put on airs, nor do they have much use for the
things that kill. They are having too much fun to worry about status
pretensions or lust for power. Rather than worship dead things, they
celebrate living things.

At the horizon of our speculations about a festive society is the development of a social philosophy of play. Wittgenstein made a distinction between "working" and "idling" language uses.[40] The festive
would likely prefer the idling languages, the expression of playfulness. Even agonistic play (debating, bartering, competing for grades
or scores or mates) would be good-natured. But they would delight in
empathic play, including storytelling, flirting, bantering, joking, kidding, intimate stroking, and lovemaking. And they would cultivate
the ultimate idling language, musement. Mulling things over is
musementive idling, or as Charles Sanders Peirce called it, "Pure
Play." Play is a "lively exercise of one's powers. Pure Play has no rules,
except this very law of liberty. It bloweth where it listeth." Musement
can take the form of "aesthetic contemplation," or "distant castle-
building," or speculation about the universe.[41] The free play of musement ponders neglected arguments, implied premises, possible explanations, indeed the infinite range of thought that leads to
hypotheses and inquiry. The mind is the elemental and maximum
field of play, where the winds of worlds real and imagined can blow,
and you can speak with any muse you wish and entertain any fantasy you desire. If there is a ludenic center in the brain, perhaps the
ultimate human festivity is the mind at play.

Yet the festive are frankly sensate, enjoying much the physical
and social pleasures of play. They are drawn to Falstaffian jollifica-
tion, seeking the fun of happy occasions and pleasant relations. However, the festive do not attach especial significance to sensual fun.
They would not constitute a "party of Eros" that sees liberation in sex
or some such. Rather, their apolitical agenda is to more broadly and
cheerfully *take it easy*. If the festive had to address the driven present
with a peroration, the message would be simple: RELAX. What the
world needs is a relaxed attitude that banishes the demons that
drive us toward more. The relaxed are willing and able to play, and to
let go of the objects of seriosity that compel us to grab and hoard. The
playful are interested in exploring what minds and bodies can experience, the joy of lex as well as the joy of sex. A relaxed attitude frees
them not only from drivenness, but also from worry. Once freed from

the domination of worry, they are able to join in the festival of life. The festive identify not with the grim Fates or avenging Furies, but rather the three Graces, who preside over the banquet, the dance, and all social enjoyments and creative arts. For them, blessed are the debonair, who live with gaiety and grace.

We may suggest here that the best human minds of the new millennium need to consider the potential for a play civilization. If play is indeed the highest expression of our humanity, can we imagine a civilization based in play? Here play would be the prime cultural enthymeme of a new culture, and reign as the mythic and basic human good on which rules, roles, and relationships are founded. In such a civilization, play would be universalized, but if everyone played, what would be the consequences? Would play be unequally distributed, or equally deserved? Would seriosity be banished, punished, or merely tolerated? How would the natural right to have fun be defined, implemented, shared, and enforced? Could a play civilization evolve into a humane and joyful Utopia, or would it deteriorate into an unfunny and anomic despot? Since a play civilization appears to be unprecedented, we may need the full power of human musement to imagine what such a world might be like, and what human possibilities might emerge from it.

As a heuristic notion, we will here suggest that any such civilization would be possible only if people developed and exercised a *comic sense of life*. Such a sensibility is contrasted to a melodramatic sense, which leads to pretensions and artifices, and a tragic sense, which leads to *hubris* and destruction. Those imbued with a sense of their own melodramatic worth or tragic destiny are oh so *serious*. The antidote against such seriosity is what literary critic Kenneth Burke called "the comic frame of motives," which act as "comic correctives." This perspective on self enables "people to *be observers of themselves, while acting*. Its ultimate goal would not be *passiveness*, but *maximum consciousness*. One would 'transcend' himself by noting his own foibles. He would provide a rationale for locating the irrational and non-rational."[42] A comic self-image allows us to see ourselves as less than aristocratic and less than heroic, and to realize what fools we mortals be. Looking at our own foolishness, we become comic critics of ourselves, making fun of our pretensions and aspirations. Comic self-criticism teaches us not to take ourselves too seriously, and indeed to enjoy ourselves in all our hilariously imperfect humanity. We become fully aware of our selves when we festively play with our selves. And what we say: Howard Nemerov, the late poet laureate, once said, "Nonsense is what we are all about." Once that is recognized, we can analyze our expressions as locations of the irrational and nonrational, of the insane inherent in the ostensibly sane, of the vast amounts of the allegedly sensible that is on reflection non-sense. Too, if play has its own truth, so do the languages of play. The playful expressions of nonsense turns serious language on its head, and that incongruity gives us new and rich perspective: the logical inversions of Lewis Carroll, the poetic punning of James Joyce, and the "fictions" of Jorge Luis Borges all offer explorations into the higher sense, or extra-sense, of nonsense. Recognizing that we are all nonsense leads us to enjoy the unending play of human Babel. One of the funniest things about us is that there is no shutting us up.[43]

The comic self observes self and world as elements of the human comedy. If there is any chance for a human corrective, it is in comic transcendence, seeing our selves and our astoundingly absurd world as if we were all part of a grand cosmic play. The Greek philosophers mused about the idea of human beings as laughing animals (*zoion gelastikon*), whose playfulness and comic sensibility were the distinguishing marks of humanity. The great essayist Montaigne preferred the comic perspective of Democritus, who found "the human state vain and ridiculous," to the serious and despairing viewpoint of Heraclitus. The human condition is such as to excite laughter at ourselves and the things we do. "There is," says Montaigne, "not so much misery in us as emptiness, not so much malice as folly. We are not so full of evil as inanity, not so wretched as we are base."[44] The key to self-knowledge and worldly wisdom is seeing us as players in the comic cavalcade of history, sharing the follies and the graces of our fellow humans, equal in our nonsense. We do not know the meaning of the whole play, but we can participate with a merry heart and sympathetic eye for that most comic of creatures, us.

One of the great students of play, Eugen Fink, noted that in the history of philosophy, thinkers have recurrently entertained the idea of defining the very meaning of existence through play. He called this "the aesthetic interpretation of the universe," the idea that somehow play explains the mysteries of cosmology: "[P]lay can become the symbolic theatrical enactment of the universe, the speculative metaphor of the world."[45] Musement on these higher meanings of play brings us breathtakingly close to metaphysics, which is beyond our competence but not beyond our ability for speculative play. And some have dared think it: in Indian philosophy, the world was created in the spirit of divine playfulness, forming the cosmic play called *lilla*; this may even be the origin of the female precursor of Eve named Lillith, who taught Adam to play, and thereby plunged the human race into *samsara*, the unending round of earthly life. This is not the cause of darkening despair but rather of eternal hope for lightening the human condition. For in this and many other traditions, there persists the ancient and enchanting thought that the gods are happiest when they see people at play.

NOTES

1. Theodore Roszak, *The Cult of Information* (Berkeley: University of California Press, 1994); Robert Everett-Green, "Information, Please," *Queen's Quarterly* 104, no. 2 (summer 1997), p. 206; William Irwin Thompson, *The American Replacement of Nature* (New York: Doubleday Currency, 1991), p. 123.

2. Don Tapscott, *Growing Up Digital: The Rise of the Net Generation* (New York: McGraw-Hill, 1998); Paul Gilster, *Digital Literacy* (New York: John Wiley & Sons, 1997).

3. Douglas Rushkoff, *Playing the Future* (New York: HarperCollins, 1996).

4. Don Martindale, *Social Life and Cultural Change* (New York: Van Nostrand, 1962).

5. Johan Huizinga, *The Waning of the Middle Ages* (New York: St. Martin's Press, 1924).

6. Umberto Eco, "The Return of the Middle Ages," in *Travels in Hyperreality* (New York: Harcourt Brace Jovanovich, 1986), pp. 59–85.

7. George F. Kennan, *Around the Cragged Hill* (New York: W. W. Norton, 1993).

8. Steven Stark, "Where The Boys Are," *Atlantic Monthly* (September 1994): pp. 18–21.

9. Johan Huizinga, *Homo Ludens: A Study of the Play Element in Culture* (Boston: Beacon Press, 1955), pp. 205–206.

10. Donald N. Wood, *Post-Intellectualism and the Decline of Democracy* (Westport, CT: Praeger, 1996).

11. Robert L. Heilbroner, *An Inquiry into the Human Prospect* (New York: W. W. Norton, 1980), pp. 158, 172–173.

12. Aldous Huxley, foreword to *Brave New World* (New York: Bantam Books, 1958), pp. xii-xiii.

13. Neil J. Smelser, "The Panic," in *Theory of Collective Behavior* (New York: The Free Press, 1962), pp. 131–161. See also Arthur Kroker et al., *Panic Encyclopedia* (New York: St. Martin's Press, 1989).

14. Gertrude Himmelfarb, *The De-Moralization of Society: From Victorian Virtues to Modern Values* (New York: Knopf, 1995); Robert Bork, *Slouching Towards Gomorrah: Modern Liberalism and American Decline* (New York: ReganBooks/Harper-Collins, 1997); Peter N. Stearns, *Battleground of Desire: The Struggle for Self-Control in Modern America* (New York: New York University Press, 1999). For a differing view, see Stepha-

nie Coontz, *The Way We Never Were: American Families and the Nostalgia Trap* (New York: Basic Books, 1992).

15. Christopher Lasch, *The Revolt of the Elites* (New York: W. W. Norton, 1995); John Kenneth Galbraith, *The Culture of Contentment* (New York: Houghton Mifflin, 1992); Charles Murray, "Of a Conservative (Created) Caste," *Harper's* (October 1991): pp. 17–18.

16. Christopher Lasch, " 'Traditional Values': Left, Right, and Wrong," *Harper's* (September 1986): pp. 13–16.

17. Burton Malkiel, *A Random Walk Down Wall Street* (New York: W. W. Norton, 1999), p. 19.

18. John R. Searle, *The Construction of Social Reality* (New York: Simon & Schuster, 1997).

19. Pierre Bourdieu, *Acts of Resistance* (New York: New Press, 1999), p. 69.

20. Richard Schickel, *D. W. Griffith: An American Life* (New York: Simon & Schuster, 1984), p. 467.

21. Harold D. Lasswell, "The Garrison State," *The American Journal of Sociology* 46 (January 1941): pp. 455–468.

22. Deborah Tannen, *The Argument Culture* (New York: Random House, 1998).

23. Murray Gell-Mann, *The Quark and the Jaguar* (New York: W. H. Freeman, 1995).

24. Stephen Toulmin, *Cosmopolis: The Hidden Agenda of Modernity* (New York: The Free Press, 1990).

25. Paul Watzlawick, et al., *Change* (New York: W. W. Norton, 1974).

26. Kevin Phillips, *Arrogant Capital* (Boston: Little, Brown, 1994).

27. Jon Katz, "The Digital Citizen," *Wired Archive* 5, no. 12 (December 1997): pp. 1–7.

28. Walter J. Ong, *Fighting for Life: Contest, Sexuality, and Consciousness* (Ithaca, NY: Cornell University Press, 1981).

29. Arthur Koestler, *The Act of Creation* (New York: Dell Laurel, 1964), pp. 27–50.

30. Samuel P. Huntington, "The Clash of Civilizations?" *Foreign Affairs* 72, no. 3 (summer 1993): pp. 22–49.

31. Jacques Ellul, "Modern Myths," *Diogenes* 23 (fall 1958): pp. 23–40.

32. Ernest Becker, *The Structure of Evil* (New York: The Free Press, 1968), pp. 169–174.

33. Richard Dawkins, *The Selfish Gene* (Oxford: Oxford University Press, 1976); Aaron Lynch, *Thought Contagion* (New York: Basic Books, 1998); J. M. Balkin, *Cultural Software* (New Haven: Yale University Press, 1999).

34. Eugen Fink, "The Oasis of Happiness," in *Game, Play, Literature*, ed. Jacques Ehrmann (Boston: Beacon Press, 1971), p. 23.

35. Hara Estroff Marano, "The Power of Play," *Psychology Today* (August 1999), pp. 36–40, 68–69.

36. George Kateb, "Utopia and the Good Life," in *Utopias and Utopian Thought*, ed. Frank E. Manuel (Boston: Beacon Press, 1966), pp. 239–259.

37. Anthony J. Celano, "Play and the Theory of Basic Human Goods," *American Philosophical Quarterly* 28, no. 2 (April 1991): pp. 137–146.

38. Gregory Bateson and Mary Catherine Bateson, *Angels Fear* (New York: Bantam Books, 1988), p. 192.

39. Conrad Hyers, "The Noblest Game: Education as Play and the Fall into Serious Work," *The Cresset* (September 1982): pp. 13–18.

40. James Guetti, *Wittgenstein and the Grammar of Literary Experience* (Athens: University of Georgia Press, 1998).

41. Charles Sanders Peirce, "Musement," in *An Introduction to the Philosophy of Charles S. Peirce*, ed. James K. Feibleman (Cambridge: MIT Press, 1970), p. 424.

42. Kenneth Burke, *Attitudes Toward History* (Boston: Beacon Press, 1961), p. 171. See also James E. Combs and Dan Nimmo, *The Comedy of Democracy* (Westport, CT: Praeger, 1996).

43. Howard Nemerov (speech presented at the Kenneth Burke Society meeting, New Harmony, IN, 1989); Susan Stewart, *Nonsense* (Baltimore: Johns Hopkins University Press, 1989).

44. Michel de Montaigne, "On Democritus and Heraclitus," in *Essays*, ed. J. M. Cohen (New York: Viking Penguin, 1958), pp. 132–133.

45. Fink, *Oasis*, p. 29.

Selected Bibliography

Ackerman, Diane. *A Natural History of the Senses*. New York: Random House, 1990.

Adair, John. *Founding Fathers: The Puritans in England and America*. London: J. M Dent & Sons, 1982.

Adams, Judith A., and Edwin J. Perkins. *The American Amusement Park Industry*. New York: Macmillan Library Reference, Twayne's Evolution of American Business Series, No. 7, 1991.

Adorno, T. W. "The Stars Down to Earth: The Los Angeles Times Astrology Column: A Study in Secondary Superstition." *Jahrbuch fuer Amerikastudien II* (1957): 19–88.

Aldrich, Nelson W., Jr. *Old Money: The Mythology of America's Upper Class*. New York: Vintage Books, 1989.

Allende, Isabel. *Aphrodite: A Memoir of the Senses*. New York: Harper-Flamingo, 1998.

Arendt, Hannah. *The Human Condition*. Chicago: University of Chicago Press, 1958.

Aron, Cindy. *Working at Playing*. New York: Oxford University Press, 1999.

Atlas, James. "The Fall of Fun." *The New Yorker* (November 18, 1996): 61–71.

Balkin, J. M. *Cultural Software*. New Haven: Yale University Press, 1999.

Barnouw, Eric. *The Magician and the Cinema*. New York: Oxford University Press, 1981.

Bateson, Gregory. "A Theory of Play and Fantasy." *Psychiatric Research Reports* 2 (1955): 39–51.

Bateson, Gregory, and Mary Catherine Bateson. *Angels Fear*. New York: Bantam Books, 1988.

Becker, Ernest. *The Structure of Evil*. New York: The Free Press, 1968.

Bell, Daniel. *The Cultural Contradictions of Capitalism*. New York: Basic Books, 1978.

Bellah, Robert N., et al. *Habits of the Heart*. Berkeley: University of California Press, 1985.

Bennett, W. Lance. "When Politics Becomes Play." *Political Behavior* 1, no. 4 (1979): 331–359.

Berlyne, D. E. "Laughter, Humor, and Play." *The Handbook of Social Psychology*, 2d ed. Vol. 3. Edited by Gardner Lindzey and Elliot Aronson. Reading, MA: Addison-Wesley, 1970.

Berne, Eric. *Games People Play*. New York: Grove Press, 1964.

Birkin, Lawrence. *Consuming Desire: Sexual Science and the Emergence of a Culture of Abundance, 1871–1914*. Ithaca, NY: Cornell University Press, 1988.

Boorstin, Daniel J. *The Image*. New York: Harper Colophon, 1964.

Bork, Robert. *Slouching Towards Gomorrah: Modern Liberalism and American Decline*. New York: ReganBooks/Harper-Collins, 1997.

Bottomore, T. B., and M. Rubel. *Karl Marx: Selected Writings*. New York: McGraw-Hill, 1956.

Bourdieu, Pierre. *Acts of Resistance*. New York: New Press, 1999.

Bright, Susie. *Full Exposure: Opening Up to Sexual Creativity and Erotic Expression*. San Francisco: Harper San Francisco, 1999.

Brown, Norman O. *Life Against Death*. Middletown, CT: Wesleyan University Press, 1959.

Bruner, Jerome, ed. *Play: Its Role in Development and Evolution*. New York: Basic Books, 1976.

Burke, Kenneth. *Attitudes Toward History*. Boston: Beacon Press, 1961.

Burns, Lee. *Busy Bodies*. New York: Norton, 1997.

Caillois, Roger. *Man, Play, and Games*. Glencoe, IL: Free Press, 1961.

Callenbach, Ernest. *Ecotopia*. Berkeley, CA: Banyan Tree Books, 1975.

Carese, James P. *Finite and Infinite Games: A Vision of Life as Play and Possibility*. New York: The Free Press, 1986.

Carey, James W. "A Cultural Approach to Communication." *Communication*, 2d ed. (1975): 1–22.

Celano, Anthony J. "Play and the Theory of Basic Human Goods." *American Philosophical Quarterly* 28, no. 2 (April 1991): 137–146.

Cherias, Jeremy, and Roger Lewin. *Not Work Alone*. Beverly Hills, CA: Sage, 1980.

Cohen, David. *The Development of Play*. Washington Square, NY: New York University Press, 1987.

Combs, James E. and Dan Nimmo. *The New Propaganda*. New York: Longman, 1993.

———. *The Comedy of Democracy*. Westport, CT: Praeger, 1996.

Combs, James E. and Michael Mansfield, eds. *Drama in Life: The Uses of Communication in Society*. New York: Hastings House, 1976.

Coontz, Stephanie. *The Way We Never Were: American Families and the Nostalgia Trap*. New York: Basic Books, 1992.

Corrigan, Robert W., ed. *Comedy: Meaning and Form*. San Francisco: Chandler, 1965.

Csikszentmihalyi, Milhaly. *Beyond Boredom and Anxiety: The Experience of Play in Work and Games*. San Francisco: Jossey-Bass, 1975.

Csikszentmihalyi, Milhaly, and Stith Bennett. "An Exploratory Model of Play." *American Anthropologist* 73, no. 1 (February 1971): 45–58.

Dahrendorf, Ralf. "The End of the 'Labor Society'. " *World Press Review* (March 1983): 27–29.

Davis, Murray S. *What's So Funny?: The Comic Conception of Culture and Society*. Chicago: University of Chicago Press, 1993.

Dawkins, Richard. *The Selfish Gene*. Oxford: Oxford University Press, 1976.

Downs, Anthony. "Why the Government Budget Is Too Small in a Democracy." *World Politics* 12, no. 4 (July 1960): 541–563.

Duncan, Hugh D. *Communication and Social Order*. New York: The Bedminster Press, 1962.

Duncan, Margaret C., et al. *Explorations in the Field of Play*. Stamford, CT: Ablex Publishing Co., 1998.

Eco, Umberto. *Travels in Hyperreality*. New York: Harcourt Brace Jovanovich, 1986.

Eco, Umberto, and Thomas A. Sebeok, eds. *The Sign of Three: Dupin, Holmes, Peirce*. Bloomington: Indiana University Press, 1983.

Edelman, Murray. *The Symbolic Uses of Politics*. Urbana: University of Illinois Press, 1967.

Edey, Maitland A., and the editors of Time-Life Books. *The Emergence of Man: The Missing Link*. New York: Time-Life Books, 1972.

Ehrmann, Jacques, ed. *Game, Play, Literature*. Boston: Beacon Press, 1971.

Eisen, George. *Children and Play in the Holocaust*. Amherst: University of Massachusetts Press, 1988.

Ellis, M. J. *Why People Play*. Englewood Cliffs, NJ: Prentice-Hall, 1973.

Ellul, Jacques. "Modern Myths." *Diogenes* 23 (fall 1958): 23–40.

———. *The Technological Society*. New York: Vintage Books, 1964.

Erikson, Erik. *Toys and Reason: Steps in the Ritualization of Reality*. New York: Norton, 1977.

Eulau, Heinz. "H. D. Lasswell's Developmental Analysis." *Western Political Quarterly* 11 (June 1958): 229–242.

Everett-Green, Robert. "Information, Please." *Queen's Quarterly* 104, no. 2 (summer 1997): 201–209.

Feibleman, James K., ed. *An Introduction to the Philosophy of Charles S. Peirce*. Cambridge: MIT Press, 1970.

Finnegan, Ruth. *Oral Poetry*. Cambridge: Cambridge University Press, 1977.

Frank, Robert. *Luxury Fever: Why Money Fails to Satisfy in an Era of Excess*. New York: The Free Press, 1999.

Frank, Robert, and Phillip Cook. *The Winner-Take-All Society*. New York: The Free Press, 1995.

Frank, Thomas. *The Conquest of Cool*. Chicago: University of Chicago Press, 1997.

Freud, Sigmund. *Civilization and Its Discontents*. New York: Norton, 1962.

Frye, Northrop. *Anatomy of Criticism*. Princeton: Princeton University Press, 1957.

Gabler, Neal. *Winchell: Gossip, Power, and the Culture of Celebrity*. New York: Knopf, 1994.

Galbraith, John Kenneth. *The Culture of Contentment*. New York: Houghton Mifflin, 1992.

Garfinkel, Harold. "Conditions of a Successful Degradation Ceremony." In *Drama in Life*, edited by James E. Combs and Michael W. Mansfield, pp. 315–321. New York: Hastings House, 1976.

Garvey, Catherine. *Play*. Cambridge: Harvard University Press, 1977.

Gaster, Theodor H. *Thespis*. New York: Norton, 1977.

Geertz, Clifford. *The Interpretation of Cultures*. New York: Basic Books, 1973.

Gell-Mann, Murray. *The Quark and the Jaguar*. New York: W. H. Freeman, 1995.

Gilster, Paul. *Digital Literacy*. New York: John Wiley & Sons, 1997.

Giroux, Henry A. *The Mouse That Roared: Disney and the End of Innocence*. Blue Ridge Summit, PA: Rowman & Littlefield, 1999.

Goffman, Erving. *Frame Analysis*. New York: Harper & Row, 1974.

———. "The Interaction Order." *American Sociological Review* 48 (1983): 1–17.

Golding, William. *The Inheritors*. New York: Harcourt Brace Harvest Books, 1963.

Goodman, Robert. *The Luck Business*. New York: The Free Press, 1995.

Gordon, W. Terrence. *Marshall McLuhan: Escape into Understanding*. New York: Basic Books, 1997.

Graham, Allison. "History, Nostaglia, and the Criminality of Popular Culture." *Georgia Review* 38, no. 2 (summer 1984): 348–364.

Groos, Karl. *The Play of Man*. New York: Arno Press, 1936.

Grover, Kathryn, ed. *Hard at Play: Leisure in America, 1840–1940*. Boston: University of Massachusetts Press, 1992.

Guetti, James. *Wittgenstein and the Grammar of Literary Experience*. Athens: University of Georgia Press, 1998.

Hans, James S. *The Play of the World*. Boston: University of Massachusetts Press, 1981.

Hays, Samuel P. "Theoretical Implications of Recent Work in the History of American Society and Politics." *History and Theory* 26, no. 1 (1987): 15–31.

Heilbroner, Robert L. *An Inquiry into the Human Prospect*. New York: W. W. Norton, 1980.

Henry, Jules. *Culture Against Man*. New York: Random House, 1963.

Himmelfarb, Gertrude. *The De-Moralization of Society: From Victorian Virtues to Modern Values*. New York: Knopf, 1995.

Hochschild, Arlie Russell. *The Time Bind: When Work Becomes Home and Home Becomes Work*. New York: Henry Holt, 1998.

Hofstadter, Douglas. *Godel, Escher, Bach: An Eternal Golden Braid*. New York: Basic Books, 1979.

Holland, Barbara. *Endangered Pleasures*. Boston: Little, Brown, 1995.

Huizinga, Johan. *The Waning of the Middle Ages*. New York: St. Martin's Press, 1924.

————. *Homo Ludens: A Study of the Play Element in Culture*. Boston: Beacon Press, 1955.

Huntington, Samuel P. "The Clash of Civilizations?" *Foreign Affairs* 72, no. 3 (summer 1993): 22–49.

Hutchinson, Peter. *Games Authors Play*. London: Methuen, 1983.

Huxley, Aldous. *Brave New World*. New York: Bantam Books, 1958.

Hyers, Conrad. "The Noblest Game: Education as Play and the Fall into Serious Work." *The Cresset* (September 1982): 13–18.

————. *The Comic Vision and the Christian Faith*. New York: Pilgrim Press, 1983.

Illich, Ivan. *Tools for Conviviality*. New York: Perennial Library, 1973.

Jewett, Robert, and John Shelton Lawrence. *The American Monomyth*, 2d ed. New York: University Press of America, 1988.

Katz, Jon. "The Digital Citizen." *Wired Archive* 5, no. 12 (December 1997): 1–7.

Kennan, George F. *Around the Cragged Hill*. New York: W. W. Norton, 1993.

King, Richard. *The Party of Eros*. Chapel Hill: University of North Carolina Press, 1972.

Klapp, Orrin. *Collective Search for Identity*. New York: Holt, Rinehart, & Winston, 1969.

————. *Inflation of Symbols*. New Brunswick, NJ: Transaction Publishers, 1991.

Klein, Richard. *Cigarettes Are Sublime*. Durham: Duke University Press, 1995.

Koestler, Arthur. *The Act of Creation*. New York: Dell Laurel, 1964.

Kroker, Arthur, et al. *Panic Encyclopedia*. New York: St. Martin's Press, 1989.

Kuentz, Jane, et. al. *Inside the Mouse: Work and Play at Disney World*. Durham: Duke University Press, 1997.

Langer, Susanne K. *Philosophy in a New Key*. New York: New American Library, 1951.

Lapham, Lewis H. *Fortune's Child*. Garden City, NY: Doubleday, 1980.

———. *Money and Class in America*. New York: Ballantine Books, 1988.

Lasch, Christopher. *The Culture of Narcissism*. New York: W. W. Norton, 1979.

———. " 'Traditional Values': Left, Right, and Wrong." *Harper's* (September 1986): 13–16.

———. *The Revolt of the Elites*. New York: W. W. Norton, 1995.

Lasswell, Harold. "The Garrison State." *The American Journal of Sociology* 46 (January 1941): 455–468.

———. "General Framework: Person, Personality, Group, Culture." In *The Analysis of Political Behavior*, edited by Harold Lasswell, pp. 200–230. New York: Oxford University Press, 1948.

Lasswell, Harold, and Abraham Kaplan. *Power and Society*. New Haven: Yale University Press, 1950.

Lears, Jackson. *Fables of Abundance*. New York: Basic Books, 1994.

Leff, Walli F., and Marilyn G. Haft. *Time Without Work*. Boston: South End Press, 1983.

Leuchtenburg, William E. *The Perils of Prosperity, 1914–1932*. Chicago: University of Chicago Press, 1958.

Levin, Harry. *Playboys and Killjoys: An Essay on the Theory and Practice of Comedy*. New York: Oxford University Press, 1987.

Lieberman, Josefa Nina. *Playfulness: Its Relationship to Imagination and Creativity*. New York: Academic Press, 1977.

Lifton, Robert Jay. *The Protean Self*. New York: Basic Books, 1993.

Lowenthal, Leo. "Biographies in Popular Magazines." *In American Social Patterns,* edited by William Petersen, pp. 63–118. Garden City, NY: Doubleday Anchor, 1956.

Lynch, Aaron. *Thought Contagion*. New York: Basic Books, 1998.

Macpherson, C. B. *The Political Theory of Possessive Individualism*. London: Oxford University Press, 1962.

Malkiel, Burton. *A Random Walk Down Wall Street*. New York: W. W. Norton, 1999.

Manning, Frank E., ed. *The World of Play*. West Point, NY: Leisure Press, 1983.

Manuel, Frank E. *Utopias and Utopian Thought*. Boston: Beacon Press, 1966.

Marano, Hara Estroff. "The Power of Play." *Psychology Today* (August 1999): 36–40, 68–69.

Marcuse, Herbert. *Eros and Civilization*. New York: Vintage Books, 1955.

Martin, Daniel. "Power Play and Party Politics: The Significance of Raving." *Journal of Popular Culture* 32, no. 4 (spring 1999): 77–99.

Martindale, Don. *Social Life and Cultural Change*. New York: Van Nostrand, 1962.

May, Lary. *Screening Out the Past*. Chicago: University of Chicago Press, 1983.

McCracken, Grant. *Culture and Consumption*. Bloomington: Indiana University Press, 1988.

McKendrick, Neil, et al. *The Birth of a Consumer Society*. London: Europa, 1982.

Mead, George Herbert. *Mind, Self, and Society*. Chicago: University of Chicago Press, 1934.

Melucci, Alberto. *The Playing Self: Power and Meaning in the Planetary Society*. Cambridge: Cambridge University Press, 1996.

Mergen, Bernard. *Play and Playthings: A Reference Guide*. Westport, CT: Greenwood Press, 1982.

Merton, Robert. *Social Theory and Social Structure*. New York: The Free Press, 1957.

Messner, Michael A. *Power at Play: Sports and the Problem of Masculinity*. Boston: Beacon Press, 1995.

Miller, David L. *Gods and Games: Towards a Theology of Play*. New York: World Publishing Co., 1970.

Miller, Perry. *Errand Into the Wilderness*. Cambridge: Harvard University Press, 1956.

Montaigne, Michel de. *Essays*, edited by J. M. Cohen. New York: Viking Penguin, 1958.

Moog, Carol. *"Are They Selling Her Lips?": Advertising and Identity*. New York: William Morrow, 1990.

Moore, Thomas. *The Soul of Sex: Cultivating Life as an Act of Love*. New York: HarperCollins, 1998.

Muller-Schwartze, Dietland, ed. *Evolution of Play Behavior*. Stroudsburg, PA: Dowden, Hutchinson, and Ross, 1978.

Mumford, Lewis. *Technics and Civilization*. New York: Harcourt, Brace & World, 1963.

Murray, Charles. "Of a Conservative (Created) Caste." *Harper's* (October 1991): 17–18.

Nasaw, David. *Going Out: The Rise and Fall of Public Amusements*. New York: Basic Books, 1997.

Ong, Walter J. *Fighting for Life: Contest, Sexuality, and Consciousness*. Ithaca, NY: Cornell University Press, 1981.

Paglia, Camille. *Sexual Personae*. New York: Vintage Books, 1990.

Paley, Vivian. *Bad Guys Don't Have Birthdays: Fantasy Play at Four*. Chicago: University of Chicago Press, 1987.

Petersen, William, ed. *American Social Patterns*. Garden City, NY: Doubleday Anchor, 1956.

Phillips, Kevin. *Arrogant Capital*. Boston: Little, Brown, 1994.

Piaget, Jean. *Play, Dreams, and Imitation in Childhood*. New York: Norton, 1962.

Polanyi, Karl. *The Great Transformation*. New York: Rinehart & Co., 1944.

Postman, Neil. *Teaching as a Conserving Activity*. New York: Dell, 1979.
————. *Amusing Ourselves to Death*. New York: Viking Penguin, 1986.
Potter, David M. *People of Plenty*. Chicago: University of Chicago Press, 1954.
Putnam, Robert D. "Bowling Alone: America's Declining Social Capital." *Current* 373 (June 1995): 3–9.
Quennell, Peter. *The Pursuit of Happiness*. London: Constable, 1988.
Rahner, Hugo. *Man at Play*. New York: Herder & Herder, 1972.
Reilly, Mary, ed. *Play as Exploratory Learning*. Beverly Hills, CA: Sage, 1975.
Rieff, Philip. *The Triumph of the Therapeutic*. New York: Harper Torchbooks, 1968.
Rifkin, Jeremy. *The End of Work*. New York: Putnam, 1996.
Robinson, Paul A. *The Freudian Left*. New York: Harper Colophon, 1969.
Rose, Arnold. *Theory and Method in the Social Sciences*. Minneapolis: University of Minnesota Press, 1954.
Roszak, Theodore. *The Making of a Counter Culture*. Garden City, NY: Doubleday Anchor, 1969.
————. *The Cult of Information*. Berkeley: University of California Press, 1994.
Rushkoff, Douglas. *Playing the Future*. New York: HarperCollins, 1996.
Rybczynski, Witold. *Waiting for the Weekend*. New York: Viking Penguin, 1991.
Sale, Kirkpatrick. *Rebels Against the Future*. Reading, MA: Addison-Wesley, 1995.
Sartre, Jean-Paul. "Beyond Bourgeois Theatre." In *Theatre in the Twentieth Century,* edited by Robert W. Corrigan, pp. 131–140. New York: Grove Press, 1963.
Schechner, Richard and Mary Schuman, eds. *Ritual, Play, and Performance*. New York: Continuum, 1976.
Schickel, Richard. *D. W. Griffith: An American Life*. New York: Simon & Schuster, 1984.
Schor, Juliet B. *The Overworked American: The Unexpected Decline of Leisure*. New York: Basic Books, 1991.
Schumpeter, Joseph A. *Capitalism, Socialism and Democracy*. New York: Harper Torchbooks, 1962.
Scott, Gini Graham. *The Power of Fantasy: Illusion and Eroticism in Everyday Life*. Diane Publishing Company, 1998.
Searle, John. *The Construction of Social Reality*. New York: Simon & Schuster, 1997.
Sennett, Richard. *The Fall of Public Man*. New York: Vintage Books, 1978.
Shames, Laurence. *The Hunger for More: Searching for Values in an Age of Greed*. New York: Vintage Books, 1991.
Shaw, David. *The Pleasure Police: How Bluenose Busybodies and Lily-Livered Alarmists Are Taking All the Fun Out of Life*. New York: Doubleday, 1998.

Showalter, Elaine. *Sexual Anarchy: Gender and Cultuire at the Fin de Siecle*. New York: Viking Penguin, 1990.

Simmel, Georg. *The Sociology of Georg Simmel*, translated and edited by Kurt H. Wolff. New York: Free Press of Glencoe, 1964.

Simmel, Georg, et al. *Essays on Sociology, Philosophy & Aesthetics*. New York: Harper Torchbooks, 1965.

Slovenko, Ralph, and James A. Knight, eds. *Motivation in Play, Games and Sports*. Springfield, IL: Charles C. Thomas, 1967.

Smelser, Neil J. *Theory of Collective Behavior*. New York: The Free Press, 1962.

Sombart, Werner. "Capitalism." *Encyclopedia of the Social Sciences*. Vol. 3, pp. 320–360. New York: MacMillan, 1933.

Spacks, Patricia Meyer. "The Necessity of Boredom." *Virginia Quarterly Review* 65, no. 4 (autumn 1989): 581–599.

Spencer, Herbert. *An Autobiography*, vol. 1. New York: D. Appleton & Co., 1904.

Stark, Steven. "Where The Boys Are." *Atlantic Monthly* (September 1994): 18–21.

Stearns, Peter N. *Battleground of Desire: The Struggle for Self-Control in Modern America*. New York: New York University Press, 1999.

Stephenson, William. *The Play Theory of Mass Communication*. Chicago: University of Chicago Press, 1967.

Stewart, Susan. *Nonsense*. Baltimore: Johns Hopkins University Press, 1989.

Suits, Bernard. *The Grasshopper: Games, Life, and Utopia*. Boston: Nonpariel, 1990.

Sutton-Smith, Brian. *Toys as Culture*. New York: Gardner, 1986.

———. *The Ambiguity of Play*. Cambridge: Harvard University Press, 1998.

Tannen, Deborah. *The Argument Culture*. New York: Random House, 1998.

Tapscott, Don. *Growing Up Digital: The Rise of the Net Generation*. New York: McGraw-Hill, 1998.

Tenner, Edward. *Why Things Bite Back: Technology and the Revenge of Unintended Consequences*. New York: Knopf, 1996.

Terr, Lenore. *Beyond Love and Work: Why Adults Need to Play*. New York: Scribner, 1999.

Thompson, E. P. *The Making of the English Working Class*. New York: Vintage Books, 1966.

Thompson, William Irwin. *The American Replacement of Nature*. New York: Doubleday Currency, 1991.

Tiger, Lionel. *The Pursuit of Pleasure*. Boston: Little, Brown, 1992.

Toulmin, Stephen. *Cosmopolis: The Hidden Agenda of Modernity*. New York: The Free Press, 1990.

Turner, Victor, ed. *Celebration: Studies in Festivity and Ritual*. Washington: Smithsonian Institution Press, 1982.

Twitchell, James B. *Carnival Culture: The Trashing of Taste in America.* New York: Columbia University Press, 1992.

————. *Lead Us Into Temptation: The Triumph of American Materialism.* New York: Columbia University Press, 1999.

Veblen, Thorstein. *The Theory of the Leisure Class.* New York: Funk and Wagnalls, n.d.

Vermorel, Fred, and Judy Vermorel, eds. *Starlust: The Secret Fantasies of Fans.* London: W. H. Allen, 1985.

Violas, Paul C. *The Training of the Urban Working Class.* Chicago: Rand-McNally, 1978.

Watzlawick, Paul, et. al. *Pragmatics of Human Communication.* New York: W. W. Norton, 1967.

————. *Change.* New York: W. W. Norton, 1974.

Weber, Max. *The Protestant Ethic and the Spirit of Capitalism.* London: George Allen and Unwin, 1930.

Wolf, Michael J. *The Entertainment Economy.* New York: Times Books, 1999.

Wolfenstein, Martha. "The Emergence of Fun Morality." *Journal of Social Issues* 7, no. 4 (1951): 10–15.

Wood, Donald N. *Post-Intellectualism and the Decline of Democracy.* Westport, CT: Praeger, 1996.

Index

About the Author

JAMES E. COMBS is Professor of Political Science Emeritus, Valparaiso University. Professor Combs is the author, editor, co-author, or coeditor of 16 earlier books, including *The Political Pundits* (Praeger, 1992) and *The Comedy of Democracy* (Praeger, 1996).